DON QUIXOTE

The Quest for Modern Fiction

TWAYNE'S MASTERWORK STUDIES

Robert Lecker, General Editor

DON QUIXOTE

The Quest for Modern Fiction

CARROLL B. JOHNSON

TWAYNE PUBLISHERS • BOSTON
A Division of G. K. Hall & Co.

Don Quixote: The Quest for Modern Fiction
Carroll B. Johnson

Twayne's Masterwork Studies No. 44

Copyright 1990 by G. K. Hall & Co.
All rights reserved.
Published by Twayne Publishers
A Division of G. K. Hall & Co.
70 Lincoln Street
Boston, Massachusetts 02111

Copyediting supervised by Barbara Sutton.
Book production by Janet Z. Reynolds.
Typeset by Huron Valley Graphics, Inc., Ann Arbor, Michigan.

Printed on permanent/durable acid-free paper
and bound in the United States of America.

Library of Congress Cataloging-in-Publication Data

Johnson, Carroll B.
    Don Quixote : the quest for modern fiction / Carroll B. Johnson.
        p.   cm.—(Twayne's masterwork studies ; no. 44)
    Includes bibliographical references.
    ISBN 0-8057-8053-X (alk. paper).—ISBN 0-8057-8103-X (pbk. :
alk. paper)
    1. Cervantes Saavedra, Miguel de, 1547–1616. Don Quixote.
I. Title. II. Series.
PQ6352.J34 1990
863'.3—dc20   89-38327
                                                          CIP

ISBN 0-8057-8053-X (alk. paper) 10 9 8 7 6 5 4 3 2 1
ISBN 0-8057-8103-X (pbk.: alk paper) 10 9 8 7 6 5 4 3 2 1
First published 1990.

for Amy

Contents

Note on the References and Acknowledgments

I have used the Norton Critical Edition's Ormsby translation of *Don Quixote*, revised and edited by Joseph R. Jones and Kenneth Douglas (New York: W.W. Norton, 1981) for all citations in the text. This translation is the smoothest and most accurate I know and is particularly useful for students because it contains excerpts from several other literary texts that constitute important background material as well as ten classic studies. Many references are simply to part (I or II) and chapter (in Arabic numerals), for example, II:14. Since the chapters are short, the passage in question can be readily located by this method in any edition.

Gustave Doré's illustrations are taken from *The History of Don Quixote*, by Cervantes, edited by J. W. Clark, with a biographical notice of Cervantes by T. Teignmouth Shore (London: Cassell, Petter, and Galpin, 1906).

I need to thank all the people who have taught me to think about Cervantes and *Don Quixote*. Some are acknowledged in the notes and bibliography, but too many are not. My teachers: Don Américo Castro, Ernest Hall Templin, Steve Gilman, Joe Silverman, Paco Márquez, Dick Andrews, Raimundo Lida. My fellow *cervantistas* and Quixote freaks: Jay Allen, Juan Bautista Avalle-Arce, Jean Canavaggio, Joaqúin Casalduero, Tony Cascardi, Anthony Close, Louis Combet, Ed Dudley, Manuel Durán, Arthur Efron, Dan Eisenberg, Ruth El Saffar, R. M. Flores, Alban Forcione, Ed Friedman, Mary Gaylord, Michael Gerli, Javier Herrero, Jim Iffland, Monique Joly, Joe Jones, Tom Lathrop, Francisco López Estrada, Howard Mancing, Mike McGaha,

Note on the References and Acknowledgments

Mauricio Molho, Luis Murillo, Jim Parr, Helena Percas de Ponseti, Richard Predmore, Augustin Redondo, Walter Reed, E. C. Riley, Elias Rivers, Elizabeth Rhodes, Harry Sieber, George Shipley, Nick Spadaccini, Bob terHorst, Alan Trueblood, Eduardo Urbina, Bruce Wardropper, Alison Weber, John Weiger, Edwin Williamson, Diana Wilson, and Françoise Zmantar. My students at UCLA, especially the ones who ask hard questions. The editor of this series and fast man with a telephone, Robert Lecker. Anne Jones and Lewis DeSimone of G.K. Hall. My analyst. My wife Leslie.

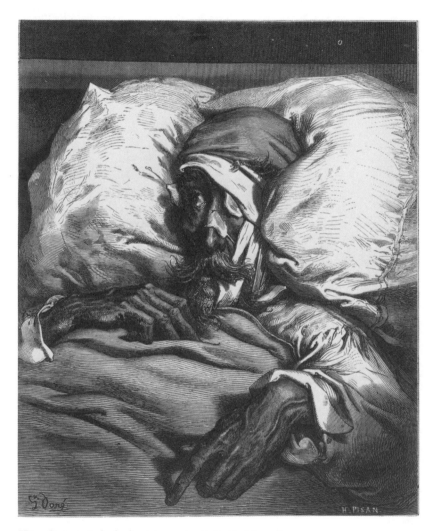

"Don Quixote in bed, about to receive Doña Rodríguez"
Illustration by Gustave Doré.

Chronology: Cervantes's Life and Works

1547	29 September? Miguel de Cervantes Saavedra is born in the university town of Alcalá de Henares, the son of Rodrigo de Cervantes, a surgeon, and his wife, Leonor de Cortinas. Fourth of a family of seven. Baptized 9 October. First Index of Prohibited Books. First Statutes of Purity of Blood.
1553	Death of François Rabelais.
1554	Publication of the first picaresque novel, *Lazarillo de Tormes.*
1556	Charles V (Carlos I of Spain), Holy Roman Emperor, abdicates in favor of his son, Philip II.
1557	Philip II's government declares bankruptcy.
1558	Death of Mary Tudor, Queen of England. She is succeeded by Elizabeth I.
1559	Publication of the first pastoral romance, Jorge de Montemayor's *La Diana.*
1561	Madrid becomes the official capital of Spain.
1563	The Council of Trent (1545–63) ends, reaffirming conservative Roman Catholic doctrine and initiating the Counter-Reformation. Birth of Lope de Vega.
1564	Birth of Shakespeare.
1565	Revolt of the Spanish provinces in the Low Countries.
1567	Publishes his first poems.
1569	In Rome, in the service of Cardinal Giulio Acquaviva; falls in love with Italian culture.
1571	The Christian fleet, commanded by Don Juan de Austria, defeats the Turks at Lepanto. Cervantes fights heroically, losing the use of his left hand.
1575	After residing in Italy for some time, sails for Spain with his brother Rodrigo on the galley *Sol.* Captured by Muslim pi-

rates, they are taken to Algiers and held for ransom. Philip II's government declares bankruptcy again.

1576   Leads the first of four unsuccessful escape attempts. Sack of Antwerp by mutinous Spanish troops, giving rise to the expression *furia española*.

1577   Rodrigo de Cervantes is ransomed out of captivity. Miguel leads another unsuccessful escape attempt.

1578   Third attempt to escape.

1579   Fourth attempt to escape. The first theaters are opened in Madrid.

1580   Is ransomed by the Trinitarian friars. Returns to Spain to find his brilliant military career is no help in securing employment. Philip II adds Portugal to his domains.

1581   Attempts a literary career in Madrid as a dramatist, without much success. Two plays date from this period: *La Numancia* and *The Ways of Algiers*.

1584   Love affair with Ana Franco de Rojas. Birth of his illegitimate daughter, Isabel de Saavedra. Marries Catalina de Salazar in Esquivias, a small town in La Mancha.

1585   Publishes his first book, a pastoral romance entitled *La Galatea*.

1587   Becomes a commissary requisitioning provisions for the Armada against England. Travels periodically from Castile to Andalucía.

1588   Defeat of the Armada.

1596   Sack of Cádiz by the English under Essex and Howard. Cervantes in business nearby in Sevilla.

1597   Collecting taxes in Andalucía. Jailed in Sevilla for irregularities in his accounts. Philip II's government declares bankruptcy again.

1598   Death of Philip II. Accession of Philip III, who turns the government over to a favorite, the Duke of Lerma.

1599   Mateo Alemán publishes *Guzmán de Alfarache I*, the classic picaresque novel. Immediate commercial success.

1601   Philip III moves the capital from Madrid to Valladolid.

1602   Cervantes's accounts investigated again. Possibly jailed.

1604   Moves with his family to Valladolid. Rumors about the loose life of his sisters and daughter. Mateo Alemán publishes *Guzmán de Alfarache II*. Peace with England.

Chronology: Cervantes's Life and Works

1605	Publishes *Don Quixote I*. Immediate success, but not as great as *Guzmán de Alfarache*.
1606	Philip III moves the capital back to Madrid.
1607	Moves with his family to Madrid.
1609	Becomes a lay brother in the Congregation of the Slaves of the Most Holy Sacrament. Loses an opportunity to return to Italy in the service of the new viceroy, the count of Lemos. Philip III's government decrees the expulsion of all the Spanish *moriscos* (Christian subjects of Moorish ethnicity).
1612	Active in Madrid literary circles.
1613	Publishes the *Exemplary Novels*, a collection of twelve short stories. From now on dedicates everything he writes to the count of Lemos. An ironic "reward" for not being included in the mission to Italy?
1614	Publishes the *Voyage to Parnassus*, an allegorical poem about literature. "Alonso Fernández de Avellaneda" publishes a false continuation of *Don Quixote*.
1615	Publishes the genuine *Don Quixote II* and *Eight Plays and Eight Interludes, Never Performed*. Philip III's daughter, Anne of Austria, marries the future Louis XIII of France.
1616	Dies in Madrid, 22 April. Death of Shakespeare.
1617	His widow publishes his last work, a Byzantine romance entitled *The Travails of Persiles and Sigismunda*.

1

Historical Context

Every book is about its own time and place. Maybe that's not what is most interesting to us in the late twentieth century, but it's a fact. Critics have always observed that Cervantes makes all the social types of his society, from prostitutes and mule drivers to ecclesiastics and the grandest aristocrats, pass in review in his pages. Yes, the *Quixote* presents a compendium of Spanish society in 1600, but that is perhaps the least profound aspect of it. Important social issues, literally matters of life and death, are taken up in the text, and Cervantes's treatment of them is characteristically antiestablishment. *Don Quixote* is a revolutionary document in its own time, a courageous piece of writing, but this important dimension is lost to us unless we can acquire some idea of the social context in which it was produced and to which it refers. Certain things in Cervantes's text make sense only within the context of the sixteenth century, and we only succeed in impoverishing ourselves and our experience if we try to pretend they're not there, or if we try to read only in terms of our own experience. We simply have to learn something about Spain between 1500 and 1615. As it happens, those were exciting times with more than a little resemblance to ours.

In my student days the first work of *Don Quixote* criticism people usually heard about was a book that appeared in 1925 by a man named Américo Castro and called *El pensamiento de Cervantes* (Cervantes's thought). Castro in 1925 saw the *Quixote* as the fruit of all the intellectual currents of the Renaissance. He demonstrates that Cervantes was at the very least abreast of what was going on elsewhere in Europe. Castro especially singles out Cervantes's familiarity with the revival of Platonism or neoplatonic philospohy in Italy, with the Italian literature of the Renaissance, and above all with the Christian humanism of Erasmus of Rotterdam.

Humanism, as the term was understood in the Renaissance, is a strategy for yielding up understanding based on the belief that the written text is the source of knowledge, and that consequently the scholar's job is to understand and elucidate the text. This is not a particularly remarkable notion in 1990. Professors of literature consider themselves humanists. Our job is to make the texts of earlier periods accessible to our students—in fact, this chapter of this book and a great deal of literary scholarship in general are examples of a degraded form of Renaissance humanism. But it was pretty revolutionary around 1450. Erasmus and his fellow humanists were practitioners and champions of what is called philology, or the New Learning. It will be helpful to consider the New Learning in opposition to its rival, the Old Learning or scholasticism.

Scholasticism considers that the process of dialectic—that is, the process of formal, logical reasoning—is the source of knowledge. Truth is arrived at, or knowledge is generated, by advancing a proposition or thesis, testing it against an antithesis, which yields a synthesis, which will in turn become a new thesis to be tested by an antithesis, and so on. This is the way that learning was carried on in the Middle Ages and into the Renaissance. Higher education was controlled by practitioners of the Old Learning. Humanism, in contrast, is based on the belief that formal logic is secondary to understanding what the text says. In order to understand what the text is saying, one needs to know the history of the language in which it is written, so that one can interpret each word according to what it meant when it was written, in the language it was written in. This is true whether one is attempting to understand a verse of the Bible or, in humanism's secular variety, a poem by Virgil or Horace. One doesn't have to be a historian of the Renaissance to know the term "secular humanism." It figures prominently in contemporary right-wing political discourse, where it is particularly charged with negative connotations. The fact that secular humanism has such a bad name now provides an excellent illustration of the process the Renaissance humanists were so concerned with. Languages have a history. The meaning of words changes over time. "Secular humanism" in the Renaissance simply meant the study of the nonreligious texts of classical antiquity as opposed to the sacred texts of Christianity. Nowadays the term means, or suggests, something far more sinister, beginning with the denial of God and culminating in a hedonistic liberalism bound to destroy society's moral fiber.

The question of humanism was no less politically charged in the Renaissance, because the Schoolmen, as the practitioners of scholasticism are called, were in control of the educational establishment as well as the ecclesiastical hierarchy, and the humanists were seen as a subversive, left-wing kind of out-group. As an example of the radically disruptive potential of humanism let us consider the case of Lorenzo Valla and the Donation of Constantine. The enormous temporal power of the papacy in Valla's day owed its legitimacy in great part to a document written in Latin and dating from the time of Constantine the Great (280?–337), which effectively ceded the entire territory of the Western Empire to Pope Sylvester I (d. 335). Valla (1407–1457) was a typical Renaissance humanist in that he was a professional student of the history of the Latin language and a crusader for a return to the purity of the linguistic practices of ancient Rome. In his *Declamatio* ("Treatise on the Donation of Constantine") of 1440 he attacked the crude Latin of the document's anonymous author and from that observation argued that it could not possibly have dated from the time of Constantine, and that consequently, it was a forgery from a much later period. By 1440 the popes' claims to temporal authority extended only to the so-called Papal States in central Italy, but Valla's exposé dramatically demonstrated how dangerous the New Learning, based on the scientific study of texts, could be to the preservation of the established order, and to all the individual careers and vested interests that went with it.

A great admirer of Valla and, like him, a professional student of the history of Latin, Erasmus (1469–1536) is best known as a Christian humanist. His work is divided into two areas. The first is the strictly professional study of texts. On the basis of his superior knowledge of the history of the languages they were written in, Erasmus made scholarly editions of important Christian writings, with the errors cleaned up and with explanatory commentary. More important for our purposes, Erasmus was also a Christian theologian in his own right. He wrote several seminal works, one in particular that had enormous repercussions in Spain due to the particular religious and social situation there. As a humanist Erasmus believed that the essence of Christianity is contained in the sacred texts, the Bible and the writings of the fathers, and not in the accumulation of traditional teachings and practices. The first duty of the Christian, therefore, is to be familiar with the text, and the first duty of the humanist is to provide a text faithful to the original, with commentary that explains the words in their historical context. The rules for being a Christian are contained in the text, and the text as Erasmus read it created a religion that was intimate and experiential, as opposed to public and participatory. Religion for Erasmus is a personal experience, and not necessarily a matter of attendance at ceremonies and participation in public rituals, parades, processions, and the repetition of prayers over and over. There are two little mottos traditionally associated with Erasmus. One is *devotio intima* (interior devotion), which simply means a turning away from the outward, public forms of religiosity in favor of a private and personal experience of some kind of communion of the believer with the Divinity. The other is *monachatus non est pietas* (the monastic state is not true piety). Erasmus held that there is no scriptural basis for the institution of monasticism, and hence, in opposition to a widely propagated belief, that being a member of the professional ecclesiastical hierarchy is no more pleasing to God than being a pious layman. This kind of result of Biblical scholarship was not likely to find favor among the members of the entrenched ecclesiastical establishment, who enjoyed a privileged status in society.

Among us English speakers the best known of Erasmus's books is probably the *Praise of Folly,* an ironic treatise in which propositions that are generally considered to be foolish turn out to be not so foolish after all. The one that was influential in Spain and has meaning for Cervantes and *Don Quixote,* is a little book called *Enchiridion militis christiani,* the *Manual of the Militant Christian.* This is where he sets forth his ideas about interior devotion, criticizing monasticism and other staples of the traditional religiosity. In the *Enchiridion* Erasmus attempts to transform the practice of Christianity from what he considered numbing ritual into a life-giving personal experience.

Why is this *Enchiridion* so important in Spain, and why do we start a chapter on *Don Quixote* by talking about Erasmus and forms of religiosity in the Renaissance? The answer lies in the historical peculiarities of Spanish society. In the Middle Ages society in Spain was organized as it was elsewhere in Europe, as a pyramid with the king at the top, the various ranks of the aristocracy coming below, along with the clergy, and the great mass of the common people forming the base. A vertical hierarchy extended upward from Bozo the Peasant through the clergy and the nobility to the King, who represented the authority of God Himself on earth. In this, Spain was like the rest of western Europe. What was unique to Spain was a simultaneous horizontal division of society into three ethnic religious groups called *castas* or castes: Christians, Muslims, and Jews. In an age when other European monarchs styled themselves "Defender of the [Christian] Faith," the king of Castile was proud to be known as "King of the Three Religions." The division of labor reflected the organization of society into these three castes. The Christians held political power. Their job was to exercise control, to make war, and to defend the country from its enemies. Those who were not members of the political hierarchy, that is, aristocrats, were generally small landowners and farmers. Moors or Muslims did all kinds of agricultural and engineering jobs, including architecture. Many of the Spanish words necessary to these professions came into the language from Arabic, because in the Middle Ages the people who did those jobs thought and spoke in Arabic. The Jews controlled the learned professions and finance. Both Muslims and Jews were active in small business. So profound was this division of labor in Castilian society that in the fifteenth century the first person one saw when entering a Christian church was a Jew, employed by the church to collect the tithes.

All this changed dramatically in 1492, when Ferdinand of Aragon and his queen Isabel of Castile, who not for nothing are known as the Catholic monarchs, eliminated the Muslims as a political entity by conquering the Moorish kingdom of Granada, and decreed uniformity of religion throughout their domains. In one stroke the old pluralistic Spain of the three religions was abolished and replaced by a monolithic society with an obligatory state religion. The Muslim population was simply subjected to forced conversion. The Jews were given the choice between continuing to be Jewish, but doing so somewhere else, or continuing to be Spanish, but doing so as Christians. Society became divided into Old Christians (those whose families had always been Christian) and New Christians (ex-Jews and their descendants, known as *conversos,* and ex-Muslims and their descendants, called *moriscos*). The traditional division of labor according to caste was preserved in a modified form. Professions and occupations that had belonged to Jews and Moors continued to be practiced by their descendants, and to be shunned by Old Christians because of their traditional associations. The Jewish merchant became the *converso* merchant. Old Christians generally stayed out of business because, to them, being a merchant meant being Jewish.

Many Jews chose to remain Jewish at the cost of leaving Spain. They emigrated all around the Mediterranean basin, taking with them the Castilian language and Spanish customs. The study of their culture into the present time is a subcategory of both Hispanic and Jewish studies. Many others, for a variety of reasons, chose to remain in their homeland and converted to Christianity. These are the ones who interest us, especially since in all probability Cervantes's forebears were among them. The sincerity and the efficacy of these conversions run the gamut from complete and utter cynicism to the most thoroughgoing fanaticism. Some people converted in order to retain control of the family business and went to Mass in public on Sunday, but continued to practice Judaism in secret on Friday night. Others ended by losing religious faith altogether. Others brought the zeal of the newly converted to the practice of their new faith with such vigor that they became the most active persecutors of the secret judaizers. The Inquisitor Tomás de Torquemada (1420–1498) is an example. Still others embraced Christianity in a different way, rose to positions of eminence within the Church and even to sainthood. The copatroness of Spain, St. Teresa of Avila (1515–1582), exemplifies this possibility. Most of the *conversos* fell between these extremes. Many if not most of these people, especially the intellectuals, were making a sincere attempt to turn Christianity from an obligatory state religion into something with some dimension of meaningful religious experience.

The presence of the first generation of *conversos*, floundering in their search for a meaningful religiosity, coincided with the appearance in Spain of the *Enchiridion*. Erasmus's little treatise on Christian piety was exactly what these New Christians needed. It showed them a form of Christianity based not on public participation in obligatory events when everyone's behavior was subject to scrutiny, but on the primacy of the Word as revealed in the sacred texts, and on the *devotio intima*, the inner experience of Divinity. This is why the *Enchiridion*, and not the *Praise of Folly*, was so popular in Spain; it meshed so perfectly with the spiritual needs of a significant segment of the *converso* population. It also begins to suggest why, by the time of Cervantes's birth in 1547, Erasmus's writings had been censored and would soon be prohibited altogether.

We have already noted the subversive potential of humanism, how Valla's study of a written text could undermine the papacy's claim to vast temporal power, for example, and how the Schoolmen, as the guardians and the beneficiaries of entrenched authority, had reason to be wary of the New Learning. In Spain the tension between the Old and the New Learning was assimilated to the division of society into Old and New Christians. There came to be an association of humanism, in particular Erasmus, with membership in the New Christian group. *Converso* intellectuals steeped in the writings of Erasmus were infiltrating the ecclesiastical as well as the temporal power structure. The very foundations of society, to say nothing of great wealth and hundreds of individual careers, were considered to be in danger.

In the year of Cervantes's birth the Old Christian majority reacted in an effort to retain control of the access to power. In that year the cardinal primate of Spain, Archbishop Juan Martínez Silíceo (1486–1557), promulgated the first Statute of Purity of Blood (*Estatuto de limpieza de sangre*) for the Cathedral of Toledo. The statute took into account the new division of society into Old and New Christians, and decreed that henceforth only Old Christian ecclesiastics could belong to the cathedral chapter, or governing body. The idea caught on immediately, and before long virtually every corporate body in which membership conferred prestige and power had adopted a similar statute. New Christians, especially *conversos,* were systematically excluded from effective participation in the power structure simply by virtue of their race. By the time Cervantes was an adult, one needed to prove "purity of blood" in order to serve on the royal councils, to be employed by the Inquisition, to belong to certain religious orders, to emigrate to America, or to belong to a *colegio mayor* (a remote ancestor of the American college fraternity). To become a member of any of the three enormously powerful military-religious orders (Santiago, Calatrava, and Alcántara) one had not only to prove purity, but also nobility of blood. By the time Cervantes was an adult a vast bureaucratic apparatus was in place to investigate the genealogies of the thousands of Spaniards who wanted to enter the multitude of organizations that required proof of racial purity, or *limpieza,* as it was known. Teams of investigators visited every town the family had ever lived in and took testimony from as many witnesses as possible, especially old people who had known the grandparents. Were the members of this family always regarded as Old Christians by their neighbors? Did they attend Mass and observe the other public practices essential to Christianity? Did they engage in any suspicious behavior, such as extinguishing the household fire on Saturday, which might suggest a clandestine observance of the Jewish sabbath? Did they show any aversion to pork? And so on. Society was divided racially, into a "pure" majority, which held power, and an "impure" minority, which was excluded *de jure* by the Statutes, and *de facto* by popular prejudice. Having the right pedigree was all-important. The affairs of the mightiest nation on earth were conducted by people whose principal qualification, in many cases, was that their family had never intermarried with Moors or Jews.

In short, Cervantes's Spain was a society in conflict, divided horizontally by a struggle between everything that was old and everything that was new. On one side stood the traditional religiosity, the Old Learning, the great mass of the Old Christian population; on the other, the new forms of spirituality championed by Erasmus, the New Learning, and the minority population of New Christians.

The traditional vertical division of society into nobility and commoners of course persisted in Cervantes's time, and this division has an immediate and lasting effect on *Don Quixote*. In Spanish, aristocrats or nobles are called *hidalgos* (literally "sons of wealth") and commoners were known as *pecheros* (literally "taxpayers"). You were born either an hidalgo or a pechero, and that was that. Your station in life, your career, and the careers of your children were all determined and mapped out in advance by the accident of birth. The concept of social mobility, which we take for granted, didn't exist, at least not officially, in Cervantes's Spain. Who you were, and what you meant in society, had very little to do with you, and much more to do with your family. You were predefined by your ancestors: by their class or either an hidalgo or a pechero, and by their caste as either an Old or a New Christian. The institutional apparatus in place was designed and organized to maintain a rigid, permanent separation between up and down, old and new.

The society that Don Quixote belongs to, at the end of the sixteenth century, might be described as one that had a particular devotion to tradition and a particular aversion to change. The forces of reaction had long since won the ideological battles. The Council of Trent (1545–64) had vigorously affirmed traditional Roman Catholic theology and practices in the face of the Protestant heresy, and Spain was the official champion of Catholic orthodoxy in Europe. Within Spain, Erasmus's works had been banned, along with many others deemed capable of stirring up the wrong kinds of thoughts. New Christians were excluded from positions of power and influence, and the centers of power were firmly in the control of the Old Christian majority. The official rhetoric exalted values, such as the traditional feudal-agrarian economy or the authority of Aristotle, over any kind of nascent capitalism or empirical science. The Inquisition was a powerful and efficient guarantor of conformity, employing drastic measures such as burnings at the stake in public "acts of faith" (*autos de fe*), and exercising absolute control over what could and could not be published. No piece of writing could see the light of day unless it had passed a rigorous ecclesiastical censorship and had been certified to contain nothing "against the faith and good customs." But there was still a dissident element in the population, composed primarily of *converso* intellectuals and businessmen who were excluded from full participation and who could not speak out openly against the official values and entrenched hierarchies. Some of these people constituted a fledgling bourgeoisie creating a stunted form of capitalism that could not compete with the systems growing up elsewhere. Others comprised a thoughtful minority within the ecclesiastical hierarchy that attempted to remain faithful to Erasmus's brand of spirituality. Still others were questioning the established values in their writings, but were doing so with extreme caution, mindful of the possible consequences of open dissent in the rigid theocracy they lived in.

This situation had immediate and important consequences for Cervantes, the kind of art he could create, and the ways he can be read. The ideological constraints imposed by his society precluded the open expression or even the suggestion of dissent. Following Erasmus and doubtless his personal inclination as well, Cervantes adopted a rhetorical strategy based on pervasive and systematic irony. Ambiguity is the watchword. The same text can be interpreted to support or to subvert the dominant ideology, depending upon the reader's own ideological orientation. This applies equally to the reader of 1600 and to the reader of 1990. One example will suffice. Around 1581 Cervantes wrote a play entitled *La Numancia,* about the heroic inhabitants of an ancient Iberian city called Numantia, who in 133 B.C. committed mass suicide rather than surrender to the Romans and come under their domination. In 1937, during the Spanish Civil War, Cervantes's play was staged in Madrid to inspire the mostly leftist, republican defenders to resist General Franco's besieging army to the last. In 1956, when Franco was in firm control, the same play was staged by his government to commemorate the victory over the defenders of Madrid in 1937. Does this play celebrate authority or resistance to authority? Clearly, it can be perceived to do either. By adopting his strategy of irony Cervantes assured the publication of a body of works with a dangerous, subversive potential in their own time, and he simultaneously assured the creation of permanently unresolvable problems of interpretation for all the generations of readers who have come along since, whose lives are not circumscribed by the oppressive realities of Spanish life in 1600.

In this context, Don Quixote's madness, his estrangement from society's norms and expectations, can mean simply an amusing inability to understand the world as it is and to recognize what is right and true. His ostracism in life and his death following the recuperation of his sanity thus constitute a clear warning to us all: Don't let this happen to you. The same character, however, can also mean a refusal to conform to a society that defines personal worth as a matter of one's ancestors and assumes the automatic superiority of Old Christians, and to a social role predetermined by one's class and caste. In this context, Don Quixote's madness can be seen as the expression of all that is new, the future instead of the past, self-creation instead of determinism, liberation instead of conformism, a slap in the face of the established order, but also the source of inevitable conflicts he is destined to lose, because he is heterodox and alone.

Many of the episodes in the novel are more or less direct reflections of the social tensions we have just seen. The reader who is unaware of how Spanish society was divided up in 1600, what the social issues were, and where Cervantes fits into the picture, can only react to them in a way that is at worst just plain wrong, and at best superficial or impoverished.

In I:4 Don Quixote sees coming toward him a group of men the narrator identifies as "some Toledo traders, on their way to buy silk at Murcia." Don Quixote stops them and orders them to confess that Dulcinea del Toboso is the fairest in the land. They object first that they do not know her, and cannot confess to what they do not know. Don Quixote insists that, without seeing her, they "believe, confess, affirm, swear, and defend" what he requires of them. This is not the language of knight errantry, but of religious conversion and instruction. The Toledo traders are being asked to believe in Dulcinea as they would believe in the divinity of Christ. The reader of 1605, a member of that society divided into Old and New Christians, would have no trouble identifying the Toledo traders as typical *converso* businessmen (because in all probability *any* businessman is a *converso*), and would consequently read their exchange with Don Quixote in terms of the tensions between Old and New. When the traders ask to see a picture of Dulcinea and then decide that "we are already so far agreed with you that even though her portrait should show her blind in one eye, and distilling vermilion and sulphur from the other, we would nevertheless, to gratify your worship, say all in her favor that you desire," they are dramatizing the process by which many *conversos* came to terms with the new, obligatory religion: just tell them what they want to hear and be left alone to attend to business. This meaning of the episode would be paramount for Cervantes's contemporaries. Our reconstruction of it here is an exercise in humanism. We are the richer because we can share the meaning enjoyed by the original readers. This does not invalidate the meaning we are most likely to find here from our twentieth-century perspective, namely that this is an episode in Don Quixote's creation of Dulcinea, as a response to and in opposition to an unacceptable vision of her offered by the Toledo traders, but we are poorer if this is all we can derive from the encounter.

In I:19 Don Quixote and Sancho are out on the road at night. They see coming toward them an apparition the narrator describes as "a great number of lights which looked exactly like stars in motion."

Historical Context

As the lights approach, they are able to make out "some twenty men in white surplices, all on horseback and with lighted torches in their hands" who "muttered to themselves in a low plaintive tone" as they came along. Behind them comes "a litter covered over with black, followed by six more mounted figures in mourning down to the very feet of their mules." Don Quixote immediately generates a fantasy to explain this apparition: the litter contains "a badly wounded knight" who needs to be avenged. Only after he has charged in and wreaked havoc do we (and he) find out that he has attacked a religious procession. How is it possible that two Spaniards such as Don Quixote and Sancho, living at a time when such processions occurred almost weekly and attendance at them was "strongly recommended," have failed to recognize the men in surplices carrying torches and praying softly as marchers in such a procession? Well, for one thing, it was dark, and for another, nobody told Don Quixote and Sancho what this really was. Our hero insists he took the marchers for "the very devils of hell," when in fact they were the opposite. Cervantes seems to be suggesting that there is no inherent difference between a religious procession and a vision out of hell. This is a scandalous proposition in the repressive environment of 1600, possible only to someone nurtured on Erasmus and his distaste for processions, someone with more than a little courage, who could furthermore put the responsibility for the scandal onto a poor psychotic who doesn't know what's what anyway. In case anyone misses the point here, Cervantes tells a modified version of substantially the same story in I:52, except that it is daylight, the procession is identified as such by the narrator, and Don Quixote is the only one who fails to identify it correctly.

In I:25 Don Quixote does penance in the wilderness for Dulcinea. He needs a rosary to aid him in his devotions, but he hasn't brought one with him, so he makes one out of his shirt tail and uses it to say "a million Avemarias." The censors were alert to the offhand reference to a million prayers, recognized in it Erasmus's aversion to the repetition of formulas, and eliminated it. They seem to have missed the more scandalous proposition, that the use of the rosary itself is either irrelevant or downright un-Christian, implied in the fact that Don Quixote fashions his rosary from what people used before the invention of toilet paper.

Early in part II there is a discussion of fame, in which Sancho urges Don Quixote to contrast some typical knightly deeds with some equally typical of sainthood. He asks, for example, whether it is better to slay a giant or to bring a corpse back to life. Don Quixote naturally allows that resuscitating the corpse confers greater fame, whereupon Sancho suggests that they give up the profession of chivalry and become saints instead. Sancho's conception of sainthood has nothing to do with sanctity or goodness or sacrifice or even just living right, but is simply the shortest route to celebrity status. "For you know, señor, the day before yesterday they canonized and beatified two little barefoot friars. It is now considered the greatest good luck to kiss or touch the iron chains with which they wrapped and tortured their bodies, and they are held in greater veneration, it is said, than the sword of Roland in the armory of our lord the king. So that, señor, it is better to be a humble little friar of no matter what order, than a valiant knight errant. With God, two dozen lashings are worth more than two thousand lance thrusts, be they given to giants, or monsters, or dragons" (II:8). Sancho's orthodoxy is impeccable. He is an eloquent spokesman for the kind of religiosity that in fact held sway in Spain, the traditional practices and values of the Old Christian majority, which Erasmus and his followers considered at best irrelevant to and at worst a mockery of Christian piety. *Monachatus non est pietas.* Read with Erasmus in mind, the speech constitutes an attack on the traditional religious practices, but if we refer it only on the ruling orthodoxy, we have a ringing affirmation of the official values.

In II:36 the duchess asks Sancho what progress he is making on the thirty-three hundred self-inflicted lashes necessary for the disenchantment of Dulcinea. He says he has made a good start, and already has five lashes administered. When she discovers he has beaten himself with his hand instead of a proper whip, she admonishes him, and reminds him that "works of charity done in a lukewarm and half-hearted way are without merit and of no avail." This talk about works of charity having merit is not the language of enchantments and knights errant, but of sixteenth-century theological debate. The censors saw in this remark an unacceptable reference to a heretical doctrine. The Council of Trent had affirmed the efficacy of works performed in whatever spirit. The important thing for Catholic orthodoxy was the work performed, and the reference to the individual's attitude was too close to Protestantism. The duchess's speech was removed. What the censors seem not to have noticed is that by talking about it in the language of contemporary theological controversy, Dulcinea's enchantment has been made analogous to another staple of Catholic orthodoxy denied by the Protestants, namely the soul in purgatory who can be ransomed out by a specified quantity or works of charity performed on its behalf by the living. Dulcinea's enchantment and disenchantment has become a gigantic parody of the institution of purgatory itself.

The theological controversies we have just seen are not the only results of the peculiar organization of Cervantes's society that find their way into *Don Quixote* and create problems of interpretation. There are other areas of concern as well. For example, the status of humanism itself is called into question in II:22, where we meet the cousin, who guides Don Quixote and Sancho to the Cave of Montesinos. This young man identifies himself as a professional humanist and states that "his pursuits and studies were writing books for the press, all of great utility and no less entertainment to the nation." His current research projects all turn out to be an unwitting parody of real humanism as we have defined it earlier in this chapter. In the time of Erasmus and Valla, humanism offered a new way of understanding man and the universe, and constituted an intellectual enterprise comparable to the discovery of the New World in physical terms. The cousin, however, is applying the New Learning to questions such as, Who was the first person in the world who caught a cold? Who was the first who used mercurial ointment as a cure for syphilis? And, he proudly states, "I quote more than twenty-five authors in proof of it." Commonsensical Sancho has this man's number. He observes that "to ask foolish questions and answer nonsense I don't have to go looking for help from my neighbors." Don Quixote immediately concurs: "There are people who wear themselves out learning and proving things that, once known and proved, are not worth a penny to understanding or to memory." From the vantage point of the late twentieth century it can be observed that anyone who has reviewed the titles of the Ph.D. dissertations submitted to any American university in any recent year will have ample reason to agree with Don Quixote. From the perspective of 1615, the episode constitutes an ironic meditation on what had happened to humanism in the preceding hundred years. The new learning had become old. It had come under the deadening influence of the prevailing mentality, and nothing had really come along to replace it. The ideological constraints of Cervantes's society assured that empirical science, the wave of the future elsewhere in Europe, would not make a ripple in Spain. The cousin still performs the classic operations of humanistic scholarship. He explicates the text and quotes more than twenty-five authors in support of his interpretation, but the subject has become trivial. Humanism subsists, but in a degraded and degenerate form.

The evolution of the Spanish economy followed the same path. The old feudal-aristocratic structures were still in place, but they had become rotted away from within. They had not been superseded by any modern economic order along capitalistic lines, nor would they be. The automatic association of involvement in business with "Jewishness" made the creation of a powerful, respectable bourgeoisie impossible. One of the episodes at the duke and duchess's addresses this issue directly. In II:48 Doña Rodríguez comes to Don Quixote by night and asks him to take a hand in the recuperation of her daughter's honor. It seems the young woman has been seduced and abandoned by one of the duke's vassals, the son of a wealthy farmer. Although the duke is acquainted with the facts, he has not forced the young man to marry the girl. Rather, he "turns a deaf ear and will scarcely listen to me; the reason being that as the deceiver's father is so rich, and lends him money, and is constantly going security for his debts, he does not like to offend or annoy him in any way." The duke is inhibited from playing his social role because he is in debt to his vassal. This deserves some exploration.

Historical Context

According to the official, visible organization of society, the duke is presumed to be automatically the most powerful because he is the richest, and he is the richest because he owns the most land. From his ownership of land flows his authority to govern, to judge, and to care for his vassals. This is feudalism functioning, and it is not for nothing that this episode is set in Aragón, the most resolutely feudal region of Spain. But something has happened here. The official and visible order has been subverted. There exists an invisible order, a deviant version of the visible one, which renders its proper operation impossible. A nonaristocrat is richer than the duke. Presumably the duke has been profligate and gone repeatedly into debt, while his vassal has been thrifty. These facts are barely alluded to in Doña Rodríguez's speech, but they are essential because they constitute a first indictment of this particular aristocrat. What we have here is an aristocrat whose wealth depends on the ownership of land (feudalism) supplanted by a commoner whose wealth is also a function of land ownership (feudalism perverted). What is missing is the bourgeois *mercader* or merchant banker, whose wealth is based on the investment of capital and operations of exchange, the wave of the future elsewhere in Europe but absent from Spain, just as experimental science was the wave of the future but is undreamed of by the cousin, who continues to practice a decadent form of humanism.

Don Quixote makes a valiant attempt to restore genuine feudalism by forcing the duke to assume his responsibility to provide justice within his domains. Doña Rodríguez presents herself in the ducal court and formally requests Don Quixote to be her daughter's champion, "because to expect that my lord the duke will do me justice is to ask for pears from the elm tree, for the reason I stated privately" (II:52). Don Quixote agrees, and then, "plucking off his glove, he threw it down in the middle of the hall, and the duke picked it up, saying that he accepted the challenge in the name of his vassal." In public, Don Quixote forces the duke to assume his responsibility by throwing down the gauntlet which the duke picks up. In private, the invisible infrastructure asserts itself. The duke naturally subverts Don Quixote's challenge, protecting the wealthy farmer and simultaneously creating a new opportunity to subject our hero to public ridicule. The official system of justice administered by the feudal lord in his domains doesn't work, and this episode, with Don Quixote's illusory success, demonstrates that it cannot be made to work. Feudalism no longer exists except in a perverted form, and the structures of Spanish society ensured that a more modern socioeconomic order would not come along to replace it.

Of course it is possible to read all the foregoing episodes solely in terms of our own twentieth-century American experience. The Toledan traders become some sane but fun-loving businessmen who give Don Quixote what he deserves and make us laugh. The religious procession becomes a mistake analogous to the windmills. Maybe we laugh at Don Quixote and maybe we feel sorry for the people he injured. Perhaps we consider how the narrator has manipulated our response (and our attitude toward crazy Don Quixote) by not telling us up front who those people really were. The significance of the shirttail rosary probably escapes us entirely because we don't know the history of toilet paper and most of us aren't Catholics anyway. The duchess's excursion into theology becomes simply another example of her gratuitous cruelty. We refer the cousin's absurd research projects to our cultural stereotypes of intellectuals in general: mad scientists and absent-minded professors. The significance of the duke's indebtedness to his own vassal gets lost because in our society there are no dukes, and being in debt is normal. It is not that we cannot relate to these episodes at all, simply that a significant possibility for experience is denied to us by our cultural deprivation. If we have no idea of Cervantes's context we cannot begin to appreciate his courage or the magnitude of his achievement, and we may conclude, with an ill-informed American critic, that his "attempts at irony are ponderous." At the very least, acquiring some knowledge of Don Quixote's society enables us to bring a more sophisticated perspective to bear on our own.

2

The Importance of the Work

Professionals of literature, and that includes both writers and critics, consider *Don Quixote* at the center of the history of the novel. The second-best-selling book in history, it includes and sums up everything that went before it, and it contains the germ of everything that's come along since. Don't take my word for it. Cervantes himself tells us it's a book made out of preexisting books. Lionel Trilling once observed that the whole history of the novel could justifiably be thought of as "a variation on the theme of *Don Quixote*." Ever since the eighteenth century writers have been creating characters who conceive some project that will give meaning to their lives, and set out to make it, and themselves, come true. From Fielding's *Tom Jones* (1749), to Goethe's *Wilhelm Meister* (1821–29), to Stendhal's *Le rouge et le noir* (1830), to *Moby Dick* (1851), to *Madame Bovary* (1857), to *Huckleberry Finn* (1885), to Philip Roth, John Irving, and Kurt Vonnegut, to Elias Canetti and Milan Kundera, novelists have been exploiting and experimenting with the possibilities inherent in what has been called "the Cervantine principle." Many writers have confessed their debt to Cervantes. Perhaps the most eloquent such confession is Flaubert's only apparently hyperbolic claim, that he discovered his own origins in the

Quixote, the book he "knew by heart before he learned to read." José Ortega y Gasset observed in 1914 that "every novel bears the *Quixote* within it like an inner filigree, just as every epic poem contains the *Iliad,* like the fruit its core." More recently (and less lyrically), René Girard has stated in an influential study of the inner structure of fiction that "all the ideas of the Western novel are present in germ in *Don Quixote.*"

The *Quixote* also resumes the existing theories of literature and anticipates all the theories and strategies of literary criticism that have come along since 1605. Every generation of intellectuals has seen its own preoccupations, and its own most cherished discoveries, anticipated in the pages of *Don Quixote.* The rationalists of the eighteenth century discovered that Cervantes had anticipated them by writing the epic of good sense and social integration. The romantics of the next century discovered the opposite, that Cervantes had anticipated their own preoccupation with the tragic situation of the eccentric genius in a hostile society. The theoreticians of literary realism discovered that he had unlocked the secret of capturing the essence of physical reality in words. In the twentieth century we have come to believe that Cervantes anticipated the existentialism of Dilthey, Heidegger, Ortega, and Sartre. All the concerns of the trendiest contemporary theorizing about literature—story and discourse, referentiality and signification, authorial voices and presences, structuralism, poststructuralism and deconstruction—can be effortlessly observed in Cervantes's pages. What is interesting is not so much the fact that the *Quixote* can be and has been profitably read and studied from each new critical perspective. That is the hallmark of any literary masterpiece: to be ahead of its time, to lend itself to new and different critical approaches, to speak to each new generation. What is truly remarkable about the *Quixote* is not that the current preoccupations are present in the text, but that Cervantes makes them themes of his work. He brings them forward consciously, as objects of inquiry, to be discussed by the characters and acted out in their lives. Another reason to read his book, then, would be for the amazingly relevant workshops it offers on literary theory and practice.

The Importance of the Work

Sigmund Freud once observed that the great writers and artists are great because they are able to intuit profound truths about human nature and human life, and to present their intuitions in a way that engages the reader's own humanity and tells him something significant about himself. In this, Freud continues, the artists and writers are way ahead of the scientists, who come to discover by rational and experimental processes what the artists already knew. Scientific discoveries form a progression in which the most recent depends on what went before. This kind of progression doesn't exist in art, except with respect to form. The intuitions of a Cervantes, or a Shakespeare, or a Rabelais are as valid for us, and as productive in our lives, as those of the most perceptive contemporary chronicler of the high tech, high crime, high anxiety world we live in. This is the best reason of all to read *Don Quixote:* to learn about ourselves and to explore our own humanity.

3

Critical Reception

In the following chapters we shall see that Cervantes introduces, worries about, and reacts to readers' and critics' reactions to *Don Quixote* all through his text. In the prologue to part I he professes to be so frightened to what people are going to say about his book that he has just about decided not to publish it at all. Once his friend convinces him to go ahead, he reminds us that from that moment on, none of us can remain neutral to it. Each of us is going to react in some way. We may get so caught up in Don Quixote's adventures that we forget to sleep, or we may throw the damn thing against the wall and go out for a beer, or anything in between. One way or another, our actions are really going to be reactions, provoked by this inanimate object. Reaction to part I is a recurring theme in part II, from Cervantes's response to Avellaneda in the prologue, to Sansón Carrasco's résumé of reader reaction in II:3, to Cide Hamete Benengeli's justification of his narrative procedures in II:44.

Because this material is organically bound to, and thematized within, the work itself, I will introduce and discuss it as I go along in the reading that follows. I hope in this way to provide some clues to a more complete understanding of what is going on and what is at stake in the book, and also to insist on the novelty of Cervantes's creation. In this chapter I want to offer a more systematic history of the text's reception, beginning with the reactions of the first readers and continuing to the present. In this chapter we'll consider the major critical statements, and I'll attempt to show how they have molded strategies of reading. We'll also see how Cervantes anticipated all or most of these reactions, from the seventeenth century to the twentieth.

James Iffland has recently written: "The spectrum of interpretations to which *Don Quixote* has given rise since its publication is very probably wider than that elicited by any other similarly well-entrenched 'literary monument' of Western culture. It should be stressed that this somewhat baldly stated claim does not center on the sheer volume of what has been written (although here, too, it would place near the top), but on its boggling diversity and contradictoriness."[1] Every possible reading has been matched by its exact contrary. The book has been read as a more or less mindless entertainment, full of comical misidentifications of reality and slapstick humor, and as a serious exploration of the most profound philosophical themes. It has been read as a cautionary tale, that is, as an example of how not to live your life: "Don't be like poor Don Quixote; he can't distinguish between fantasy and reality. He makes a fool of himself. His death is a triumph because he finally gives up his craziness and joins society." It has been read as a positive example of moral greatness in a degraded and decadent society: "If only there could be a few more Don Quixotes, the world would be a better place. His death is a tragedy because it means that the idealism has been beaten out of him." The book has been hailed as a shining example of Renaissance humanism, a celebration of the spirit of reason, and as its polar opposite, a fictionalized treatise on the reactionary theology adopted by the Council of Trent. It is the first modern novel. No, it is the last medieval romance. No, it is a kind of halfway point in the evolution of romance into novel. Cervantes says it's just a satire of the romances of chivalry, and he ought to know. As a matter of fact, Cervantes had no idea what he was writing about; it's much more than a literary satire, but it wrote itself in spite of Cervantes. No, Cervantes was the most self-conscious writer who ever put pen to paper; he knew exactly what he was doing at all times. It is a book about books and reading. It is a book about chivalry. It celebrates chivalry. It ridicules chivalry. It contains a revolutionary social message. No, it celebrates the feudal social order and the role of the aristocracy.

Marthe Robert concludes: "After more than three centuries of critical and scholarly effort to establish the definitive meaning of *Don Quixote,* we are still uncertain how to approach the work."[2] To become a reader of *Don Quixote* is to be forced to take a position, to become a participant in a spirited polemic that sometimes even takes on the aspect of a life-and-death struggle. Cervantes knew this was how it was going to be when he wrote the prologue to part I in 1605, not because he could predict the future, but because, like all great writers, he knew a lot about people. J. J. Allen points out in *Don Quixote, Hero or Fool?* (1969) that readers and critics have always tended to line up to one side or the other. You are either with Don Quixote (he's a hero) or against him (a fool). I would add that we also line up according to our idea of Cervantes. He is either a spokesman for the official values of his society, or he is a critic. The question is, how do we come to hold these opinions? Why should we care whether Don Quixote is a hero or a fool, or what Cervantes's cultural politics were?

Cervantes's deceptively modest declared intentions are not much help. He tells us in the prologue to part I that he is offering a simple literary satire, or as he puts it, an "invective" against the romances of chivalry. Some critics, including some writing now, would like to base their reading entirely on Cervantes's statements. This view runs the risk of reducing the *Quixote* to an old book about some other old books that nobody has cared anything about for hundreds of years. The fact that we still read *Don Quixote* and become passionately involved with it suggests that there must be considerably more to it than Cervantes allows to meet the eye. Of course, the reader who is familiar with the romances of chivalry can appreciate Cervantes's parody of that genre and its conventions, and his experience with the *Quixote* is consequently enriched. Similarly, we can appreciate the social dimension of the text through an exercise of humanistic scholarship, but we cannot experience it as Cervantes's contemporaries did because we are products of the twentieth century.

The reaction of those contemporaries is best summed up in a story about King Philip III of Spain (d. 1621) himself. On overhearing a student laughing uproariously at something, the monarch quipped: "Either that young man has taken leave of his senses, or he is reading *Don Quixote*."[3] Peter E. Russell explains: "For more than one and one-half centuries after the book was first published, readers, not only in Spain but in all Europe, apparently accepted without cavil that *Don Quixote* was simply a brilliantly successful funny book." Laughter was considered therapeutic, and "Cervantes certainly had this curative function of laughter in mind." "Cervantes and his contemporaries had views about what was funny which differed in various respects from ours: an ugly or distorted face, an inept physical action, a silly word, a wine of unpleasant taste or a rose with an unpleasant odour. Insanity, provided it was not too violent, was funny." The early readers identified with society rather than with Don Quixote. According to Renaissance theory, comedy is in fact based on the audience's distance from, as opposed to identification with, the characters and their mishaps.[4]

The rationalists of the eighteenth century read the *Quixote* as a commentary on the relation between madness and society. Don Quixote's madness is defined as a rupture with the norm, a flight from reason, a refusal to see things as they are, for which he is roundly, repeatedly, and justly punished. The book becomes the epic of reason and adaptation to society's norms. This reading has made a major comeback in the last twenty years or so, possibly as a reaction on the part of certain readers and critics to a society that appears to teeter on the brink of cultural anarchy by fostering dangerously permissive habits of thought.

Around the end of the eighteenth century certain philosophers became interested in what we would nowadays call the problem of individual human identity, or selfhood, or personhood. In the process they discovered the dialectic of self and society. One of the first of these philosophers was Johann Gottlieb Fichte (1762–1814). Fichte maintained that "the self presents itself . . . in the form of an individual will that needs outside resistance in order to continue to operate. The self cannot become independent without resistance." In France, Pierre Maine de Biran (1766–1829) laid particular stress on the conscious effort of the will to impose itself on circumstance. "Liberty," he writes, "is nothing less than the experience of our activity or of our power to act and to create, the constituent effort of the self."[5] Europeans who had been exposed to this idea that the self realizes itself struggling against the resistances that allow it to continue being could begin to read *Don Quixote* in a new way. If Don Quixote himself personifies the self in this dialectical relationship, the stage is set to regard him more sympathetically than people were used to, thus preparing the way for the Romantic revolution in interpretation.

This reading strategy has dominated reaction to *Don Quixote* since the beginning of the nineteenth century. It offers two major breaks with what had gone before. First, Don Quixote the character is seen to incarnate certain values. He stands for something, and the sane and straight society in which he struggles to exist stands for something else. The text thus becomes the story of a clash of universal values. In fact, the greatest theorist of the German Romantic movement, Friedrich Wilhelm von Schelling (1775–1854) wrote in 1802 that "until now, we have had only two novels: Cervantes's *Don Quixote* and Goethe's *Wilhelm Meister*." Of the *Quixote* he says: "The theme of the whole is the Real in conflict with the ideal."[6] The *Quixote* thus becomes a work of universal philosophical import, by definition no longer a funny book, but a profoundly serious one. The second break lies in the reversal of the reader's identification. In the Age of Reason, readers had identified with society's norms. Now, for the first time, Don Quixote becomes the sympathetic focus of attention. The romantic writers saw him as a version of themselves, a being morally and artistically superior to his environment, but tragically doomed to be misunderstood, derided, and finally crushed by an unfeeling society. His struggle is seen as noble, the more noble precisely because it is foredoomed to failure. Furthermore, the ironic stance from which the hero is portrayed suggested to these writers a form of what has been called "romantic irony," in which the artist mocks his own most cherished illusions.

Most if not all modern readers, and virtually all of the legions who have only heard about *Don Quixote* second hand, bring the residue of the romantic interpretation to their experience of Cervantes's book. The enormously popular musical *Man of La Mancha* (1966) is a good example of this tendency. It is a degraded version of the desire to see in Don Quixote a sympathetic figure of tragic grandeur, and not simply an old fool, because he dares to dream the impossible dream and is destroyed for his idealism. James Iffland evokes a whole "legion of modern heroes in literature and film whose inner projects propel them straight into the face of an uncomprehending 'society,'—either to be destroyed (*One Flew over the Cuckoo's Nest*) or to triumph (*Fitzcarraldo*)."[7] This notion of an "inner project" that gives meaning to one's life is fundamental to our twentieth-century experience. We can trace its beginnings to such forerunners of Romanticism as Fichte and Maine de Biran. It has been systematically elaborated in the philosophical writings of Alfred Adler (1870–1937), José Ortega y Gasset (1883–1955), and Jean-Paul Sartre (1905–80), and unconsciously absorbed by the rest of us. When we see Don Quixote formulating his project and literally willing himself into existence in the very first chapter of the novel, it is easy to conclude that Cervantes has anticipated our twentieth-century view of man in society, and that he thinks like we do.

The major critical statements since 1900 have in the main been reworkings of the Romantic interpretation. Arthur Efron has recently offered a useful expansion of this category into what he calls the "idealist" position. "In the most pervasive of all approaches to *Don Quixote*, the Knight is regarded as being in some sense the locus of positive value. Depending on the critic and the period in which he writes, Don Quixote may be described in positive terms because of his role as restorer of traditional cultural values, or because of his idealistic opposition to the values of his social environment, or because he is seen as an example of modern rather than medieval man, creating his individual personality with the strength of his own will and imagination rather than carrying out the role that his society had defined for him."[8]

Probably the most extreme example of this position is the one taken by the Spanish philosopher Miguel de Unamuno (1865–1936). In an influential book called *La vida de don Quijote y Sancho, escrita por Miguel de Cervantes y explicada por Miguel de Unamuno* (The life of Don Quixote and Sancho, written by Miguel de Cervantes and explained by Miguel de Unamuno) (1905), he comes to regard Don Quixote as the incarnation of all that is noble in the Spanish soul. He goes so far as to view the hero as a kind of Spanish Christ, crucified by a Spain that didn't understand who he was or what his presence in the world meant. Unamuno exalts the hero's irrationality as well as his latent capacity for mobilizing others by the example of his devotion to a cause.

A much more scholarly variation of the idealist approach is *El pensamiento de Cervantes* (Cervantes's thought) (1925), by Américo Castro (1885–1972). Castro is reacting to an almost universally held belief (promulgated especially by Unamuno) to the effect that Cervantes had written a masterpiece almost by accident, without really knowing what he was doing. He demonstrates with a wealth of documentation that the reverse is true. Cervantes was at the very least abreast of the intellectual developments in sixteenth-century Europe, he swam easily in the currents of Renaissance humanism, and he was heavily influenced by Erasmus. In this he formed part of a rationalist intellectual minority in his society, still committed to the concepts of received truth and ecclesiastical authority. He cloaked his radical critique of Spanish society in more or less pious hypocrisy. That last word has got Castro into lots of trouble over the years, especially with his fellow Spaniards, who naturally want to claim Cervantes as the leading national genius but can't stand the idea that he might have been playing games with the national values. Even critics who reject the later evolution of Castro's thought (and they are many) regard *El pensamiento de Cervantes* as the definitive characterization of Cervantes as a man of the Renaissance. Alban Forcione has recently continued this line of investigation in a series of splendid studies of Cervantes's *Novelas ejemplares* (Exemplary tales) (1613) and the posthumous *Trabajos de Persiles y Sigismunda* (Travails of Persiles and Sigismunda) (1617).[9]

Explication of the novel in terms of the periods of cultural history is not without contradiction. If in 1925 Castro considers the *Quixote* a kind of compendium of the Renaissance and the ideology of humanism, Joaquin Casalduero in 1949 sees in it the esthetic of the Baroque and the ideology of the Council of Trent.[10] Casalduero reads in light of the principles of art history established by Heinrich Wölfflin (1864–1945), for whom Baroque art is characterized by a "disordered order." An apparently senseless maze is in fact a carefully worked out complex structure where the details serve a greater unity. The structure of the art work acts out the organization of the world as posited by Counter-Reformation theology: a tangle of apparent contradictions that masks God's essential order.

In 1926 a book appeared by the Spanish scholar and diplomat Salvador de Madariaga, entitled *Guia de lector del Quijote* (English translation *"Don Quixote": An Introductory Essay in Psychology*, 1935). This work has the merit of treating Don Quixote and the other characters as though they were real people whose behavior can be analyzed using the methods of modern psychology. This book has been followed by other explorations of the characters' psyches, notably from a Jungian perspective by John G. Weiger,[11] Freudian analysis tempered by American ego psychology by C. B. Johnson,[12] Jungian analysis tempered by contemporary feminist theory by Ruth El Saffar,[13] and the wildest of them all, the unsettling psychosexual ambiguities proposed by Louis Combet.[14]

Américo Castro left Spain at the end of the Spanish Civil War. From his new vantage point at Princeton University, he offered in 1948 a radical new interpretation of Spanish history based on the fact of seven hundred years' cohabitation of the Iberian peninsula by three ethnic-religious communities: Christians, Moors, and Jews.[15] Around 1500, as we have seen, the old distinctions were obliterated and replaced by the division of society into Old and New Christians, ushering in what Castro called "the Age of Conflict." Castro based all his subsequent writings on Cervantes on the subterranean social tensions he had discovered in Spanish life. In a succession of important studies listed in the bibliography, Castro considers both Don Quixote and his creator sympathetically and positively as men profoundly out of tune with their society, and seeks to read the novel from within the unique dialectic of Spanish life. These studies tend not to be taken as seriously as they should be in the English-speaking world, but Castro is being rediscovered by his countrymen and by the continental European intellectual community. The most accessible of Castro's "new" *Quixote* studies is the "Introduction to *Don Quixote*" which appears in the volume *An Idea of History: Selected Essays of Américo Castro* edited by Stephen Gilman and Edmund King (1977). This general line of inquiry has been fruitfully continued by Francisco Márquez Villanueva and Joseph Silverman,[16] among others.

The more dispassionate versions of the idealist reading are often modified into what Efron calls the "perspectivist" school. "Here the critics refuse to see Cervantes or the novel as endorsing either the real or the ideal, but find that the novel shows an inevitable tension between these two perspectives, each of which appears in some way to have its claim to being an ultimate reality, and each of which is interpreted as part of the inherent human condition. Perspectivism ultimately assumes that life is the interplay of a number of equally real levels of reality."[17] The notion of such an interplay is generally associated with the Spanish philosopher José Ortega y Gasset. In 1914 Ortega published an influential book entitled *Meditaciones del Quijote* (English translation: *Meditations on Quixote,* 1961) in which this concept, of such obvious and fundamental relevance for Cervantes, is offered as a key to understanding. Virtually everyone is willing to see a clash of differing perspectives in, for example, Don Quixote and Sancho and their discussions of windmills and giants. Some critics do take Cervantes's central thesis to be that meaning resides not in the thing contemplated, but in the beholder, who necessarily comes to grips with reality from his own unique perspective. The notions of interpretative codes and semiotic processes, which will figure so prominently in my chapter on readers and reading, provide a modern conceptual support for the perspectivist view. In practice, however, critics tend to want to come down on one side or the other. Manuel Durán's *La ambigüedad en el Quijote* (Ambiguity in the *Quixote*, 1960) is probably the "purest" example of the perspectivist stance. Américo Castro might be described as a perspectivist who tends to identify with Don Quixote against society. On the other hand, Juan Bautista Avalle-Arce, the author of many influential studies on *Don Quixote* and first president of the Cervantes Society of America, is a perspectivist who finally comes down on the side of society.

Those who take a hard line with respect to Don Quixote, who identify instead with society and its norms, fall into what Efron calls the "cautionary" group, which he describes as

> a less popular stream of criticism that has taken Don Quixote for a man with good intentions that require purification under the pressure of reality. The proponents of this view do not dismiss or minimize his errors of perception, but concentrate upon the impurity of his ideal; Don Quixote exhibits certain suspect traits, such as the urge for fame and the tendency to dictate an irrelevant idealism out of the past onto his own world. In this view, characters like the Priest, the Canon, and the Man in Green often serve to suggest a realistic standard of values and become standard-bearers of the author's viewpoint as well as of the Counter Reformation, to whose values the author is assumed to have subscribed. Slowly in the course of the novel Don Quixote is brought to realize the truth and beauty of this realistic norm, and at his death—a favorite scene for this approach to the novel—he fully accepts it.[18]

This approach, which harks back to the Age of Reason, is enjoying a renaissance of popularity, especially in the English-speaking world, thanks principally to the influence exerted by Anthony Close's study *The Romantic Approach to Don Quixote* (1977). Close contends that the Romantics simply misunderstood Cervantes's text by bringing anachronistic notions of the relation of self and society to their reading. He seeks to undo what he regards as centuries of persistent and widespread error and restore the meaning the text must have had for Cervantes and his contemporaries. Other critics particularly associated with this point of view are P. E. Russell and, with reservations, Daniel Eisenberg. Many of the most interesting and penetrating recent studies begin with or come to espouse the "hard line," although frequently their interest (for me, at any rate) does not reside in their attitude toward the hero. You need to read Daniel Eisenberg and Edwin Williamson,[19] for instance, to understand chivalry and the appeal of chivalric romance. Alban Forcione's continuing exploration of Cervantes's humanism is extremely enlightening, even if it is not based on any particular sympathy with Don Quixote or a view of his author as nonconformist. Ruth El Saffar's incisive early, formalist studies have been followed by exciting readings from feminist and Jungian perspectives, which incidentally suggest a growing sympathy toward Don Quixote.[20]

At the risk of failing to mention many other important critics and their readings, I must bring this survey of critical reception to a close. I have tried to suggest here that there is not and cannot be a single "correct" interpretation of *Don Quixote*. The book is to us as the windmills or the barber's basin are to its characters; it means what we need it to mean, according to what we want/need Don Quixote and Cervantes to be. Something in the text, whether it's the protagonist's grandly futile efforts, or the society that ultimately brings him into the fold, or something else, reaches out and hooks a part of our psyche. The American psychoanalytic critic Norman Holland has referred to this as touching the reader's own unconscious "identity theme."[21] The French Marxist theoretician Louis Althusser calls the same unconscious process "interpellation." The text literally hails the reader, calls out to him as a member of a class, a community, existing at a particular time and shaped by certain particular historical forces.[22] The book's meaning is the consequence of this meeting of what's in the text with what's in the reader: historical situation, education, life experience, hopes, fears, desires, projects. Our experience with any literary text, therefore, is really our experience with ourselves, at a particular moment in our lives. We do not merely read the text; the text has the power to read us. It makes us see things about ourselves that we hadn't been aware of before. What is unique about *Don Quixote,* I believe, is that Cervantes had figured all this out in 1605 and wrote a book about it.

a reading

"Don Quixote and the windmills"
Illustration by Gustave Doré.

4

What Happens in *Don Quixote I* (1605)?

A Revolutionary Prologue

English translations of Cervantes's prologue begin by addressing us as "idle reader," suggesting that our idleness, our boredom, is about to be relieved by the story he is going to tell us. The usual translation of the Spanish *desocupado lector* is misleading. Cervantes's Spanish does not evoke a state of idle boredom, but the absence of engagement. The unengaged reader is at loose ends, not presently involved with anything that claims his attention. Cervantes is going to do something not for us but to us. His first words draw us into an obligatory relationship with the text we have before us. From now on we are no longer *desocupado*, or unengaged, but locked into a relationship with this text. We can continue reading, or we can put the book down, or we can throw it against the wall. What we do doesn't matter as much as the fact that we must do something. We can no longer remain neutral; we have to react in some way. The text has in fact engaged us. Whatever we do, we do because the book has made us do it. Every text has this property; Cervantes is the first author in European literature to call attention to it and to make an issue of it.

Now that he has our attention, Cervantes proposes for our consideration an analogy between the author of a literary work and the father of a child. The analogy is not original with him. In fact, it was a staple of sixteenth-century prologue writing. The typical author addresses the reader, tells him the text is his "child," the offspring of his imagination, and identifies with the text as the parent identifies with his or her child. More often than not, this identification includes an exercise in false modesty. The "parent" pretends to believe that the "child" is deficient in some way and begs the reader to overlook the faults he finds. This, Cervantes declares, is exactly what he will not do. He invokes the standard analogy only in order to distance himself from it. He identifies himself not as Don Quixote's father, but his stepfather. He thus steps away from that direct parental involvement in what the world may think of his little darling, declaring in effect that he really doesn't care what we think of this book.

Having distanced himself from his creation, Cervantes then insists on his inability to influence our reaction to it and our opinion of it. He reminds us that each one of us is alone with the text, in the privacy of our own home. There is no public opinion here, as there is in the theater, for example, to monitor our reactions and make sure we laugh at the appropriate places, or that our reaction in general conforms to accepted standards of behavior and commonly held values. All this, he says, "frees and exempts" us from having to react to this text in any particular way. What Cervantes does not say, but what is implicit in this passage, is that our freedom is in fact an enormous responsibility. If the author can't control our reaction, and doesn't care what we think anyway, and if there is no one else around to tell us what to think, we have to think for ourselves. We are free, but that means that we are not free not to react, to form opinions, to make judgments. We are, as Cervantes insinuated in his first words to us, engaged with this text.

Now Cervantes begins to tell us how this book is different from other books, and because he is Cervantes, he does it by telling us a story, in which he himself is a character. He is concerned that *Don Quixote* does not have any laudatory poems at the beginning written by famous writers or important politicians. It has no citations from famous authors or sacred scripture, to be identified in marginal notes. It has no explanatory notes relating to historical events or geography or any other branch of learning. And last but not least, it has no bibliography of works consulted. Cervantes professes to be so worried about his book's shortcomings that he has just about decided not to publish it at all. At this point he describes himself, seated at his desk, his paper before him, his pen behind his ear, his elbow on the desk and his cheek in his hand, thinking how he can write an acceptable prologue to such a deficient book, when a friend walks into his study and engages him in conversation. After listening to Cervantes's recital of his book's deficiencies, the anonymous friend attacks them one by one and either explains them away or proposes remedies. The poems at the beginning can be supplied by some Cervantes can write himself and attribute to whomever he likes. If he wants marginal notes, he can put into the text a reference to something everyone already knows, or to a text everyone has already read, then annotate away. As for a bibliography, he can lift one intact from some other book and drop it in whole, with every entry from *A* to *Z*, pertinent or not. Who reads the bibliography anyway, and if someone should read it and believes Cervantes actually used all the works cited, he is a fool who gets what he deserves. It turns out that the things Cervantes's book lacks are unnecessary. What appears to be a confession of deficiency, how this book suffers by comparison to all the others that are being published, is in fact an advertisement of originality. Cervantes modestly attributes this advertisement to his friend, distancing himself even from the solution to his own "problem."

This book is not like other books. It does not rely on authority but on its own originality. Similarly, this prologue is not like other prologues. Instead of identifying with his work and pleading with us to like it, Cervantes distances himself from it and tells us we have to make up our own minds. Each one of us is alone with the text, from now on.

INTRODUCTION OF THE PROTAGONIST: I:1

The text begins by calling attention to itself as a text, based on archive research and on preexisting accounts. The narrator refers, for example, to "those who have written on the subject," and to "all the inhabitants of the district of the Campo de Montiel" who knew the hero. This implies, and we are also told, that the story we are going to read is true. Its hero is an anonymous country gentleman (*hidalgo*) whose name might be Quixada or maybe Quexana, who lived "not long ago" in a real place somewhere in La Mancha whose name the narrator declines to state. Our hidalgo has only two suits of clothes, one for weekdays and one for Sundays. His diet repeats itself week after week, year after year. Like every other member of his social class, he does not work, but lives off the meager revenues from his modest land holdings. For diversion, he hunts. He is a bachelor, about fifty years old, who lives with a housekeeper about his own age and a niece just under twenty. He has two friends, the parish priest and the village barber.

The only thing that distinguishes him from thousands of other country hidalgos is his passion for reading. Something in his immediate environment drives him to immerse himself in a kind of escapist fiction not unlike the James Bond stories or the Rambo films, to the point of losing his grip on reality. Day and night, he abandons himself to what are called romances of chivalry, enormously popular adventure books about knights errant and their ladies fair. He finally loses touch with reality, withdraws into psychosis and in this new state conceives a project that will give meaning to his life: to become a knight-errant and actually live out a chivalrous adventure story like the ones he spends all his time reading. The books will provide a script, or at least a scenario, on which he can base his life. Phrased another way, his life will be an imitation of art. This project also implies, for the first time, an identity, embodied in the name Don Quixote de la Mancha. It takes him a week to think of this name. By naming himself, Don Quixote literally wills himself into existence. The anonymous hidalgo is gone, but the named character who replaces him really doesn't have an identity—yet. He has, or rather he *is*, the potential for an identity, a name setting out to become an identity. Names are enormously important in this book, and naming is one of the principal activities the characters engage in. Naming is a process that moves in two directions. Projected from inside the individual, the name announces to the world who he thinks he is, or wants to be. Imposed from without, the name designates what or who the world thinks the person is or wants him to be. Sometimes this coincides with the identity the individual is trying to project; sometimes it doesn't. Nobody can really believe he is who he thinks he is unless the world, the Other, validates his identity by reflecting it back on to him, crystallized in the name he calls himself. This is what the existentialists mean when they say that man is that being who has no being, that the being of each of us resides not in ourselves but in the Other. Becoming who we want to be implies forcing the Other to recognize us as such. This is the task that confronts Don Quixote as he sets out to live the life of a knight errant, to come to the aid of damsels in distress, to battle giants and other evildoers, to redress grievances and right wrongs. It will not be easy, for the identity he has chosen is anachronistic in the late sixteenth century, and the world can only recognize him as a madman. He naturally surrounds himself with the trappings of knight errantry: armor and a horse. But all he can produce is an outdated suit of armor left over from his grandfather's time with a partly homemade helmet, and a skinny nag he has imaginatively promoted to the status of warhorse simply by renaming it. The figure Don Quixote cuts is doubly ridiculous: anachronistic to begin with and a grotesque deformation of what a knight should have looked like a hundred years before.

There is a final item of equipment he needs in order to complete his outfit: a lady fair. It seems the exercise of chivalry has two aspects. There is the obvious aggressive dimension involved in slaying giants and jousting with other knights, and there is also an amorous-erotic aspect. To be a knight errant was to be simultaneously a fighter and a lover. Don Quixote needs someone in whose name he will perform his great deeds of chivalry, to whom he will commend himself before entering battle, to whom he will send those he vanquishes, who will be constantly in his thoughts and to whom his heart will be pledged. Don Quixote has no wife, and the only women in his life are his niece and his housekeeper. He had once been in love with a farm girl from neighboring El Toboso, but his attentions seem to have been limited to worshiping her from afar, because she wasn't aware of his interest in her. He decides to make her the "lady of his thoughts," to promote her to the cateogry of chivalric princess as he had promoted his horse, by renaming her. Aldonza Lorenzo becomes Dulcinea del Toboso.

Our hero has now generated three names: his horse's, his lady's, and his own. Since he himself attaches great importance to them we should consider their various significances. The name *Rocinante* is composed of two Spanish words, *rocín* and *ante*. *Rocín* is defined in a Spanish dictionary of 1611 as "an old, worn out horse, useless as a mount for the nobility and for war," what we would call a nag. The word *ante* means "before." Hence *Rocinante* means "that horse who was a *nag before,* and who is now *before* all the other *nags* in the world." Don Quixote himself explicates the hidden meaning of his horse's name, and in so doing invites us to ponder the others he has invented.

His own name takes him eight days to invent, and it incorporates a wealth of allusion. To begin, our hero promotes himself from the class of hidalgo (the lowest rung of the nobility) to that of caballero by calling himself *don*. Now, this word *caballero* has two meanings. With respect to the real society of 1600, inhabited by Cervantes as well as by Don Quixote, a caballero is the second lowest member of the hierarchy of aristocrats. A caballero owns more land than an hidalgo, he owns a horse (a *caballo*, not a *rocín*), and he is entitled to use the honorific title *don* before his name. With respect to the tradition of chivalric literature in which Don Quixote immerses himself in his readings, a caballero is a knight errant, a knight in shining armor, an old-fashioned kind of literary character. The misadjustment between literature and life that will characterize Don Quixote begins here, with this *don* that pulls him back into the reality of Spain in 1600 even as he attempts to escape into literature.

The name *Quixote* is most probably derived from the Catalan word *quixot,* designating a piece of armor that covered the thigh. An appropriate enough association, it would seem, although not particularly ennobling. In addition, the name *Don Quixote* rhymes with and sounds very much like *Lanzarote* or Lancelot, King Arthur's champion and one of the greatest heroes of knight errantry. Don Quixote is not unaware of this association. He makes use of it in chapter 2 when he assimilates himself to Lancelot by substituting *Don Quixote* for *Lanzarote* as he quotes an old ballad. Alas, the name *Don Quixote* also recalls a certain *Camilote*, a comic knight errant who appears in one of the books Don Quixote loves to read and makes a fool of himself in public. The noble, positive associations present in *Don Quixote-Lanzarote* are called into question by those lurking in *Don Quixote-Camilote*.

Finally, since our hero's most admired model was a knight named Amadís *de Gaula* (from Wales), he resolves to follow the example by incorporating his homeland into his name as well, calling himself Don Quixote *de la Mancha*. Unfortunately, the associations are not the same. Gaula is exotic, a place of mystery, associated with both the Carolingian (about Charlemagne) and the Arthurian cycles of chivalric fiction, a kind of mythic homeland of all the values of chivalry. *La Mancha*, on the other hand, is a word that means "stain" in Spanish, and is the name of a region with nothing particular to recommend it: no cities, no illustrious families, the site of no important historical events, a semiarid plain given over mostly to wheat and dotted with windmills. To be from La Mancha was distinctly not an honor, the exact opposite of being from Gaula.

The name Don Quixote gives his lady fair is similarly complex. *Dulcinea* is clearly derived from the adjective *dulce*, "sweet." It is based more immediately on a shepherd named Dulcineo who appears in a book by Antonio de Lofrasso called *Las fortunas de amor* (The fortunes of love, 1573). This book belongs to the pastoral tradition, whose theme is love. The name of Don Quixote's lady love, then, could not be more appropriate. Like his own, it harks back to a particular form of literature with particularly significant and positive associations. Like his own, it also includes a reference to its bearer's homeland, and this reference undercuts the positive values present in the rest of it. El Toboso is a town in La Mancha which was remarkable in Cervantes's time chiefly because it was populated almost entirely by *moriscos,* the descendants of Moors forcibly converted to Christianity around 1500. It was a place of supremely negative associations in a society dominated by devotion to the concept of racial purity.

All these names are a study in ambiguity, a mixture of serious and comic literature set into a relationship with life, in which the liberating, universalizing tendency of literature is mocked and undone by the presence of prosaic historical reality. There is no need to wait for the introduction of Sancho Panza to observe the clash between the universal and the particular, poetic fiction and history, spirit and matter. These contrasts are present from the very beginning, in the names Don Quixote gives himself, his horse, and his lady.

THE FIRST SALLY: I:2–5

Don Quixote sets out on his adventures one hot July morning. He is alone with his thoughts, and as he rides along he fantasizes not only the great deeds he is to perform, but also the record of those deeds, his history or *historia,* which he assumes will be written down by a "sage magician." He even imagines the text of the magician's narration of what he is doing at that moment. Don Quixote invents a narrator who takes him seriously and praises him. We know, but he does not, that his deeds are in fact already being narrated, and that the narrator thinks he is a fool. While Don Quixote's fantasy narrator speaks of the "renowned knight," and his "celebrated steed," the real one observes that the sun was hot enough "to melt his brains, if he had any." Because we know more than Don Quixote does about what is happening to him, it is easy for us to feel superior to him. In fact, the narrator invites us to do just that by establishing such a violent contrast between the character's comically mistaken idea of what is going on and what we know to be true. This relationship to the character, known as "dramatic irony," governs our perception of Don Quixote's first sally.

Our hero makes his first stop at a country inn. The narrator tells us it is an inn, but Don Quixote thinks it is a castle like the ones in his books. Why does he misapprehend reality in this way? For one thing, knights-errant do not operate in inns. In order to behave like a knight-errant, Don Quixote needs a knight errant's environment. This means he needs to transform the inn imaginatively into a castle. He imposes his will on a prosaic reality in order to create the environment he needs in order to be who he wants to be. His madness is what allows him to work this transformation and to believe in it. Most of the rest of us know, for example, that however much we wish our VW were a Maserati, wishing will not make it so. Psychotic people, however, regularly deploy an ego defense known as "distortion," defined as "grossly reshaping external reality to conform to inner needs." Through distortion, a VW can really be experienced as a Maserati. It is important to observe that only psychotics engage in this behavior. This is exactly what Don Quixote does, and this is one of the things that allows us to identify him as a psychotic. Conversely, the fact that this is an unconscious psychic process and not a willful, conscious act of imagination is what guarantees that for Don Quixote, that large building out there really is a castle. We will have much more to say about the process of interpreting reality later on. It is important to understand from the beginning, however, that Don Quixote is not playing games.

Our hero begins to interact with reality at this inn that for him is a castle. He cuts a ridiculous figure in his antiquated armor and makeshift helmet, and he affects the archaic speech of the romances of chivalry. He identifies himself in effect as a living anachronism, a madman, but nobody present at the inn attempts to bring him to sanity or even to contradict him. Everyone decides instead to humor him. The innkeeper and two prostitutes who happen to be in residence play along with his strange perceptions and behavior. The innkeeper even dubs him knight in a burlesque ceremony. Don Quixote thus has no difficulty in reshaping external reality to conform to his inner needs. The result, for him, is a clear validation of his existential project by the Other. The world treats him as he thinks he ought to be treated, on the basis of who he thinks he is. For Don Quixote, his brief sojourn at this inn is a triumph. For us, it is a sequence of hilarious mismatches between what Don Quixote thinks is the meaning of what is happening to him and what we know (because the narrator tells us) is the real

DON QUIXOTE

meaning of the same events. Our enjoyment is derived from the fact that we know more about his situation than he does.

When Don Quixote sets out from the inn, now "officially" a knight, he has two adventures. One is a triumph and the other his first defeat. He comes upon a boy tied to a tree and being beaten by his master, a job for a knight errant if there ever was one. He intervenes on the boy's behalf and forces his master to stop beating him and to pay him what he owes him. Off he goes, feeling good about himself and about knight errantry. He does not know that as soon as he is out of sight the master starts in again on the boy, only this time with more feeling. In fact, our hero's intervention has been counterproductive. Once again our enjoyment of this episode is a result of our knowing what he does not. Once again, we are invited to see him as a fool.

Shortly thereafter he encounters a group of traders on their way to Murcia to buy silk. He has no idea who they might be, nor does he care. They exist for him as an invitation to act out a typical kind of episode in imitation of his chivalry books. He stations himself in the road, stops the group and challenges them to confess that Dulcinea del Toboso is the fairest in the land. When they refuse, and then make fun of him besides, he attacks. He winds up in a position that will become typical, stretched out on the ground, his body bruised and his lance broken. A kindly neighbor happens by and takes him home, slung over Rocinante's back.

AT HOME: I:6–7

Chapter 6 is devoted to an examination of Don Quixote's books by his friends, the priest and the barber. Several romances of chivalry, as well as other varieties of fiction such as pastoral romances, are passed in review and commented upon. A few are saved, but most are condemned to be burned. This episode combines literary criticism with a parody of the practices of the Inquisition. Don Quixote is asleep while this is going on. When he wakes up his niece explains the disappearance of his library by telling him that an enchanter (a typical character in the romances of chivalry) had whisked everything away, books, room and all, in a cloud of fire. This turns out to be bad therapy, because it gives Don Quixote a ready-made explanation, which he will invoke from now on, of why the world isn't the way he thinks it is. The same enchanter who stole his books continues to pursue him, changing reality around to make him look bad, to be defeated in battle, and so on. This explanation is indisputable because it is not the product of Don Quixote's disordered mind, but of the sane and straight society around him.

In chapter 7 Don Quixote equips himself with the one additional item of equipment a knight-errant must have: a squire. He chooses a peasant from his village named Sancho Panza. Sancho is everything Don Quixote is not, and vice versa. Everybody, including people who have never read the book, knows that Don Quixote is tall and thin, Sancho short and fat. The word *panza* means "pot belly" in Spanish. Don Quixote is a very minor aristocrat, Sancho a commoner. Don Quixote is a great reader. In fact, this is what makes him Don Quixote. Sancho is illiterate. Furthermore, he has never heard of romances of chivalry. Don Quixote belongs to the culture of literacy, whose medium is the written word. He understands and explains the world through what he has read, especially his beloved romances of chivalry. Sancho belongs to the culture of orality. He opposes the great body of folk wisdom crystallized in proverbs to Don Quixote's reliance on written texts.

Professional *Quixote* scholars have related the Quixote-Sancho pair to the traditional characters of Lent and Carnival, the one a thin figure mounted on a scrawny horse, the other jolly and rotund, surrounded by all the good things to eat that Lent forbids. Carnival means literally "good-bye to meat." This pair particularizes, within the context of Christianity, the universal polarity between the upper and lower halves of the human body. The bottom half is where the organs of digestion, excretion and generation are located. A character associated with this region, one named "pot belly," for example, is in effect a celebration of our sensory, sensuous, and sensual nature. He stands in opposition to a figure associated with the head, with reason, control of the passions, and with the denial of the "lower" functions. We like to think that our humanity consists largely in the domination of our appetites and gross physical functions by our minds, and most of the time this is so. But at Carnival time the normal hierarchical relation is inverted, and for a few days the lower half is master. Mardi Gras at New Orleans is a direct survivor of this tradition. It retains its link to the liturgical calendar in that it still coincides with the beginning of Lent. Spring break at Fort Lauderdale (or whatever the in spot is this year) is a secularized version of the same temporary celebration of our "baser" appetites.

There was also an Italian comedy team popular in the late sixteenth century composed of Bottarga (a fat man) and Ganassa (a thin one), easily referable to Carnival and Lent and the rich folkloric tradition that goes with them. Cervantes was undoubtedly familiar with both. Sancho and Don Quixote certainly exploit the comic possibilities inherent in the fat-thin pair. As their perceptions and personalities bounce off each other, Don Quixote and Sancho can be uproariously funny, but they are more than a sixteenth-century Laurel and Hardy. It is because all these pairs dramatize the warring impulses within each of us that they keep recurring and are so easy to identify with. They exist in uncomical form in Cooper's Natty Bumppo and Chingachgook, in Melville's Ishmael and Queequeg, in Mark Twain's Huck Finn and Jim, in Steinbeck's George and Lenny. Finally, and this is most important for our reading of Cervantes's text, Don Quixote and Sancho are two complex characters, fictional people who act astonishingly like real people, an improbable male couple thrown together in situations that force them to come to terms with each other and make a life together. What is narrated in the text is the evolution of their friendship, their reciprocal effect on each other, their mutual bonding.

This is not to say that Sancho and Don Quixote have nothing at all in common at the start. It is easy to get carried away with the symbolic or allegorical dimension of their respective characteristics and to fail to observe, for example, that both men are about the same age, that they are leaving houses dominated by women, and that they are going off in search of something better, or more exciting, or more rewarding. Don Quixote is after fame, to be won by his deeds as a knight. Sancho is in it for an *ínsula* that Don Quixote has promised him. Now *ínsula* was an archaic word in Cervantes's time, found only in old books like the romances of chivalry. By 1600 it had been superseded by the modern *isla,* "island." It is hard to believe that Sancho has any idea what an *ínsula* might be, except an excuse to get him out of the house. That is, it is highly likely that Sancho's motivation to go off with Don Quixote has more to do with what he is getting away from than what he may be getting into. Similarly, we have already noted that something, we know not what, in Don Quixote's homelife, had driven him to his massive reading of escapist fiction in the first place, and finally to seek refuge in madness. These shared similarities underlie the differences we have noted above. Although we may not be immediately aware of them, they help us to experience Don Quixote and Sancho as complex, verisimilar characters, and they certainly facilitate the process of bonding that occurs between them.

THE SECOND SALLY: I:8–52

When Don Quixote sets out again it is with Sancho. He will of course be engaged in the necessary activity of reshaping external reality to conform to his inner needs, but from now on it will be immensely more difficult for him to do so. This new difficulty is the real theme of the paradigmatic Don Quixote adventure, the one that gave the phrase "tilting at windmills" to our language. It is easy for Don Quixote to convince himself that those gigantic figures up ahead with the huge whirling arms are a band of lawless giants with whom he must do battle. His psychosis in fact ensures such an interpretation. The problem is to convince Sancho. Sancho is outside Don Quixote. He is the Other, and he is right there, immediately present. He has to be dealt with. He does not share Don Quixote's perception of the world for two reasons. First, he is ignorant of chivalric romances and the importance of giants in them, and second, he isn't crazy. He has no need to interpret reality except in the prosaic sense he is used to. In fact, he cannot see things any other way. Don Quixote and Sancho act out the phenomenon known in *Quixote* criticism as *perspectivism*. This means simply that Cervantes demonstrates, over and over again, that each individual necessarily interprets and comes to grips with reality from his own unique perspective: who he is, what his experiences have been, what his needs are, what he is carrying around inside him. So when Sancho asks Don Quixote: "What giants?" that most innocent of questions signals a radical rupture with the past, and the beginning of a new period in both his own and his master's life. For Don Quixote, the enterprise of Being is suddenly subject to massive new obstacles. It is no longer possible, as it was when he was alone, simply to read reality in terms of his books of chivalry and act in consequence. For Sancho, it means trying to understand a new way of relating to the world, totally alien to his experience. From now on, it is in every sense a "new ballgame." Fortunately, Don Quixote has recently been provided with a splendid new tool to help him deal with Sancho's obstinacy. When Sancho refuses to see giants, and when Don Quixote is flat on his back after attacking windmills, he falls back on the explanation so graciously provided by his niece. The same enchanter who spirited away his library caused the giants to be changed into windmills just when he was attacking, in order to rob him of the victory. This allows him to simultaneously have his giants and to agree with Sancho about the windmills.

Immediately after the adventure of the windmills, Don Quixote runs into a Basque gentleman escorting a lady in a carriage. Imposing a chivalresque fantasy on this appearance, he concludes that the lady is being taken somewhere against her will, and that the intervention of a knight-errant is urgently required. He and the Basque come to blows, but right in the middle of their combat the narrative stops. We are now told that what we have been reading is the transcription of a text by someone referred to as the "first author," who had compiled it on the basis of archive research, previously existing written accounts, and interviews with the inhabitants of La Mancha who had known Don Quixote. The narrative we are reading must stop because the first author's manuscript ends here. Our concern is wrenched violently away from the outcome of the battle between Don Quixote and the Basque, and transferred to the problem of the text itself. Our narrator, who calls himself, logically enough, the "second author," now relates his serendipitous discovery of a new manuscript containing the remainder of the story of Don Quixote. But this new text, welcome as it is, is fraught with problems. It is the work of an Arab historian named Cide Hamete Benengeli. We are reminded that Arabs are not to be trusted in general. In particular, Benengeli can be assumed to be hostile to a Christian knight such as Don Quixote, and we can therefore not trust him to relate our hero's glorious deeds in all their glory. Finally, Benengeli's Arabic text must be translated into Castilian, which necessitates the services of a bilingual *morisco* youth the "second author" contracts to do the job. From now on the text we read will be the second author's transcription (with commentary) of the bilingual youth's translation of Cide Hamete Benengeli's Arabic manuscript.

From now on there will also be two great themes to claim our attention. We already know about the story of Don Quixote and Sancho, and we naturally want it to continue. We might call this story the "fiction." In addition, Cervantes has now created a metafiction, a story about someone called the "second author" and the production of the text he offers us. From now on this book will be the story of the fictional protagonists and what happens to them, and a meditation on the nature and mode of existence of a literary text. That is, the book will be simultaneously about Don Quixote and about itself.

Modern readers tend to find the metafiction more interesting than the fiction. It involves the most fundamental preoccupations of literary theory, beginning with a radical questioning of the premises of the *Poetics* of Aristotle (384–322 B.C.), and it lends itself to analysis from the trendiest contemporary perspectives. Furthermore, such analyses are immensely rewarding. We shall have a great deal more to say about these matters. For now we need to keep in mind that *Don Quixote* is the first work of Western literature to display this obsessive concern for literary theory, that makes the discussion of theory part of the practice.

In chapter 16, fresh from a battle with some disgruntled herdsmen, Don Quixote and Sancho find themselves at the inn of a certain Juan Palomeque. It is an important locale to which they will return later for an extended period (I:32–46). Don Quixote naturally interprets the inn as a castle, and on this first visit he falls in love with Palomeque's attractive daughter, whom he naturally mistakes for the daughter of the aristocratic castellan (castle keeper) he naturally mistakes Palomeque for. He is awake in his bed working on an erotic fantasy about her, when squat, ugly Maritornes the servant enters the room on her way to a tryst with one of the mule drivers. In one of his greatest triumphs of distortion, Don Quixote overrides all his sense perceptions and imposes on Maritornes all the attributes of Miss Palomeque, herself metamorphosed into an aristocrat. His speech to the stunned Maritornes is all about how flattered he is that she has offered herself to him, and how he cannot accept because his heart is pledged to Dulcinea del Toboso. This encounter, which ends in a brawl involving everyone present, is one of the great comic scenes in literature. Besides amusing us, it tells us something about Don Quixote that might have escaped us. He is strongly attracted to women and terrified of them at the same time. We also see that Dulcinea is not just another item of knightly equipment, but that she can be mobilized to form a barrier between Don Quixote's desires and his fear of having to act on them.

The following morning Sancho is tossed in a blanket by Palomeque and his friends because Don Quixote had naturally refused to pay for his lodging. No knight in chivalric romance ever paid for a night in a castle, he reasoned. With that our two heroes are on the road again. There follows in swift succession a series of adventures that all have to do with the interpretation of reality by Don Quixote and by Sancho. At stake in every case is first the meaning of whatever it is that's out there, and then the effect of the two different interpretations on the relationship between the two characters. The narrator also plays on our relationship to these sights and sounds, by sometimes giving us all the information we need to make our own interpretation and sometimes withholding essential data, leaving us to flounder with Don Quixote and Sancho. This series of "mistaken identity" adventures forms the narrative backbone of part I. These episodes are what most readers remember best. After the mixup at Palomeque's come: the flocks of sheep/armies (I:18), the nocturnal religious procession (I:19), the noise of the fulling mills (I:20), the barber's basin/enchanted helmet (I:21), and the liberation of the galley slaves (I:22). The basin/helmet reappears in I:45, where its meaning is finally verified by the democratic process. (Democracy isn't necessarily the solution to everything.) We shall have a great deal more to say about this theme of the interpretation of reality. For now it is more important to point out that what is at stake here is not the essence of the objects under discussion, but their meaning. There is never any real doubt, for example, that the windmills are windmills. The question is, rather, What do they mean? to Don Quixote? to Sancho? And most important of all, what kind of interpretative codes does each interpreter use in order to arrive at his intepretation? These interpretations do not take place in a vacuum but involve clashes of different individual perspectives. The culmination of this series of episodes occurs in the combined discussion of the barber's basin and his mule's packsaddle in I:45. The whole question of the meaning of the objects is finally subordinated to the interpersonal relationship of the two protagonists.

Alongside the series of adventures of interpretation of reality is another in which Don Quixote and Sancho are more passive, reduced in some cases to the roles of observers or listeners. They are known collectively as the "interpolated stories," and they are all about love. In chapter 11 Don Quixote and Sancho fall in with some goatherds. They introduce them to the story of a certain Grisóstomo, who has killed himself for love of the beautiful Marcela. Later they become peripherally involved in the tangled love affairs of Luscinda and Cardenio, and Dorotea and Don Fernando. In chapter 32 everyone assembles again at Palomeque's inn, including Don Quixote's friends the priest and the barber, who have come out to find him and bring him home. They meet a middle-aged soldier who has escaped captivity in Algiers in the company of a beautiful Moorish woman, and hear the story of his adventures. The innkeeper produces "The Tale of Foolish Curiosity," a manuscript left by some previous guest. It is the story of a bizarre love triangle in Italy, which is read aloud to the assembled company. Don Quixote sleeps through this one, awakening only to engage in a short but fierce combat with Palomeque's supply of red wine, stored in huge wineskins that he interprets as giants. The captive soldier's brother, a judge, shows up with his daughter. She is being trailed by a young swain who overtakes her at the inn, where their amorous situation is resolved. On their way home they meet another goatherd, who tells the story of his own unfortunate experience in love.

Everyone has a story to tell, and every time someone tells a story it is immediately subjected to critical commentary by those present. Sometimes the mere mention of literature is enough to set off a discussion. There is an extended one at Palomeque's inn (I:32) regarding the historical accuracy and the literary merit of Don Quixote's favorite reading, the romances of chivalry. Everyone present, the innkeeper himself, his wife, their daughter, Maritornes the servant, Dorotea, and the priest, is vitally involved with the books of chivalry from his/her own unique perspective. Everyone expresses an opinion. The question, like the matter of physical reality, comes to be not so much about the nature of those books, but about their meaning to those present and their effect upon the lives of the people who read them.

After the liberation of the galley slaves (I:22) and before everyone reassembles at Palomeque's inn (I:32), Don Quixote and Sancho take refuge in the rugged mountains in Sierra Morena. What our hero considers a noble act of setting people free who are being held against their will is considered by the state to be a criminal offense. Hence the prudent withdrawal into rough terrain. Finding himself in the wilds, and having just met Cardenio, who has gone crazy and taken refuge there because he could not deal adequately with the demands of his love life, Don Quixote decides to go crazy himself (I:25). He will imitate simultaneously an episode from *Amadís de Gaula* and another one from *Orlando furioso,* performing all sorts of crazy antics while doing penance for Dulcinea. He will send Sancho with a letter to her, describing his piteous state and urging her to have mercy on him. In the course of their conversation Sancho discovers the relation between

Dulcinea and Aldonza Lorenzo, whom he knows well. This is a real crisis in the viability of the myth of Dulcinea, and we will say more about it later. Sancho sets out for El Toboso, but he never arrives there because he meets the priest and the barber, out looking for Don Quixote. When he and his master are reunited, Don Quixote naturally wants to know what happened in El Toboso. Of course Sancho can't tell him the truth, so he tells him another story (I:30), in which he superimposes everything he knows about Aldonza onto Dulcinea. In order to save Dulcinea from degenerating into Aldonza Lorenzo, Don Quixote has to "rectify" practically everything Sancho tells him. The scene is hilarious but also serious, because it reconvenes the workshop in narrative theory. Among the topics treated: the relation between truth and verisimilitude, history and poetry, the priority of story over discourse, the generation of discourse from a mental construct, the dialogue of narrator and narratee.

We shall consider these issues systematically later on. For now we need to note that Sancho outdoes himself as a storyteller. He tells Don Quixote that Dulcinea is not amused by his antics and requests him to report to her in El Toboso. This is a real crisis in her continued viability. From Sancho's perspective, if they actually go to El Toboso he will be caught in his lie. From Don Quixote's, going to El Toboso can only result in a confrontation with Aldonza, and if he could confront Aldonza, he would never have needed to invent Dulcinea in the first place. To go to El Toboso would be intolerable for both Don Quixote and Sancho. Fortunately our hero has a prior commitment that prevents him from honoring Dulcinea's request. The crisis is averted, for the present. It will reappear, and be played out, at the beginning of part II.

By now everyone is back at Palomeque's inn. The various love stories are resolved. The problem of interpretation of reality is resolved (more or less) as the episode of the barber's basin/enchanted helmet and mule's packsaddle/warhorse's trappings is finally concluded (I:45). In the end, the question of the objects' essence is subordinated to the relations that individual characters establish with them and with each other. A plan is conceived to get Don Quixote home by convincing him he has been enchanted and locking him in a cage, then transporting the cage back to the village on an ox cart (I:46). On the road home the company meets a canon, an ecclesiastical dignitary from Toledo, who engages both the priest and Don Quixote in another round of literary discussions (I:47–48, 50). To the canon's impeccable Aristotelian theory Don Quixote opposes the extemporaneous invention of an exciting episode in the style of the romances of chivalry, together with a moving summary of how his life has been changed, how he is a better person, for having read those pernicious books. It becomes clear that there is more here than the simple condemnation of a certain kind of reading material. Once again, the focus comes to rest on the personal involvement of the individual reader with the text, and on the relation between reading and living.

In chapter 52 Don Quixote reaches his village. It is Sunday, everyone is out in the plaza, and our hero is forced to make a humiliating grand entrance in his cage. Both he and Sancho repair to their respective homes. Sancho demonstrates what he has learned, or how he has changed, as a result of his close association with Don Quixote. When his wife asks him what he has brought her, he replies that nothing material can compare with the thrill of adventure and the expectation of what is to come. In the word coined by Salvador de Madariaga, Sancho has become *quixotized*. Don Quixote is greeted by his niece and housekeeper and put to bed. There is a promise of future adventures.

The text ends as it began, by calling attention to itself and to the labors of the second author to bring it to light. The second author also relates how he found the record of Don Quixote's third sally, thus strongly insinuating the publication of a second part.

5

What Happens in *Don Quixote II* (1615)?

MORE STRANGE PRELIMINARIES

Ten years elapsed between the publication of parts I and II. In that time Cervantes became an important writer, never completely accepted by the reigning literary lions, but definitely a presence on the Madrid scene. The introductory material to part II is a reflection of his status in the literary world of 1615. *Don Quixote I* was an enormous popular success and in 1614 had spawned an illegitimate sequel by an anonymous author who signed himself Alonso Fernández de Avellaneda. In his prologue to the reader Cervantes subjects Avellaneda's continuation to an attack of withering sarcasm. He takes Avellaneda to task for calling him old, remarking that "one writes not with gray hairs but with the intellect, which normally improves with age." He tells a couple of anecdotes in which the hapless Avellaneda is compared to a particularly bizarre madman. Within the text, beginning in II:59, he will destroy the bogus characters and their author by absorbing them into his own fiction.

In his dedication of part II to the count of Lemos Cervantes also indulges in some fairly heavy-handed sarcasm toward his patron. Because Lemos had not included him in his retinue when he became viceroy of Naples in 1609, Cervantes facetiously dedicated to him everything he wrote from that time forth, always loading his dedications with lavish praise and thanks for apparently nonexistent favors. He tells Lemos, for example, that *Don Quixote* is popular even in China, and that the emperor of China has offered to make him the head of a new university there, but that he prefers to enjoy the "patronage" of Lemos from nearby Naples. The reader can perceive that Cervantes is in Madrid, instead of with Lemos in Italy, and draw his own conclusions.

Even the ecclesiastical approbation of this book is unusual. Although signed by a certain Licenciado Márquez Torres, it echoes the things Cervantes says about himself in his dedication to Lemos and in his prologue to the reader. In a typically Cervantine way, by telling a story, it paints a moving portrait of Cervantes as the outstanding Spanish writer of his time, clearly superior to all his contemporaries and yet tragically unrecompensed for his gifts to humanity and his service to his country.

BEFORE THE THIRD SALLY: II:1–7

Within the fiction, only one month has elapsed since the end of the second sally, but things have evolved. First, the anonymous hidalgo of I:1 has actually become Don Quixote. The narrator and the other characters never call him anything but "Don Quixote." During the course of part I he has literally formed himself, by constantly making decisions, by choosing to do one thing and not another. These choices form a pattern that has come to define him as a person. Phrased another way, Don Quixote now has a history, and through it a character. This fact makes it harder for him to be Don Quixote now that it was in part I, because the range of possibilities for action is narrowed. We readers can imagine him doing certain things but not others. We expect him to be psychotic, and we expect him to be in love with Dulcinea, for example, but we would be surprised and suspicious if he were to get drunk and tell off-color stories. Don Quixote now has to act in character, be true to himself, or forfeit our interest in him.

What Happens in Don Quixote II *(1615)?*

The semiotic theme of interpretation of reality so prominent in part I gives way to part II to an interest in Don Quixote himself and especially in his madness. Is he crazy or isn't he, and if he is, in what does his madness consist? These are the questions the priest and the barber attempt to answer when they call on their friend in II:1. The matter is more complex than we might think. They (and we) learn that he is lucid and eloquent on every subject except chivalry, but even this monomania is not entirely straightforward. Don Quixote is aware of himself as an anachronism. He knows he does not inhabit the late medieval world of chivalry, but insists that the decadent times he does live in cry out for a revival of the chivalric spirit. He has come a long way from the almost mechanical, gross reshapings of exterior reality to conform to inner needs that we observed in the early chapters of part I. On the other hand, his physical symptoms still point to madness. When his friends enter his room they find him "so withered and dried up that he looked like a mummy." Don Quixote is still crazy. His craziness is an essential part of his identity, one of the things that define him as Don Quixote, but here in part II there is a new emphasis on the complexity of his madness.

A new character, a recent university graduate named Bachelor Sansón Carrasco, is introduced here. He will carry on in part II some of the functions the priest had in part I. He will come after Don Quixote and try to get him to return to the village, for example. But there is an essential difference between his character and the priest's. Like many other prople here in part II, Sansón is something of a prankster and practical joker. He is not above making fun of Don Quixote.

His first mission is to notify Don Quixote and Sancho that a book has been published that recounts their exploits. The seminar on literary theory and practice is reopened, in a new and more complex context. Our heroes are now simultaneously "real" people (in a verisimilar text) and characters in a work of literature (*Don Quixote I*) that we have read and that appears as such in the work we are now reading (*Don Quixote II*), in which they are "real." In part I society was divided into those who read the romances of chivalry and those who don't; in part II the division is between those who have read *Don Quixote I* and those who haven't. Here in part II, part I performs the functions that preexisting literature in general, and especially the romances of chivalry, performed in part I. Part I will be subjected to critical commentary, as we shall see in a moment, and part I will influence the actions not only of Don Quixote but of many other characters as well. Furthermore, there has also appeared another *Don Quixote II* not written by Cide Hamete Benengeli, so Sancho and Don Quixote are also the genuine, authentic, originals, as opposed to the imitation versions in the other book.

Don Quixote's knowledge of his fame has now caught up with ours. We have always known that the chronicler of his deeds is the "Arabic and Manchegan historian, Cide Hamete Benengeli," but until now Don Quixote has been fantasizing an entirely different kind of historian. Now he understands that the creation of his public person is in the hands of a writer who may be inimical to him. That is, he becomes aware, as we have already been made aware, of the problems posed by the presence of a narrator who mediates experience and reception. The text of *Don Quixote I* is passed in review by Sansón at Don Quixote's request. That is, Cervantes takes the opportunity not just to criticize his own text, which he did throughout part I, but to incorporate real reactions to part I and subject them to his own commentary. Our hero is concerned to know which of his adventures are considered the best. Sansón's answer is a kind of summary of Cervantes's artistic credo: "In this matter there are different opinions, because people's tastes are not the same." Everyone reacts on the basis of who he is, what his experience has been, what his desires are. When we read, we read ourselves. There is a brief discussion of the standard Aristotelian topics: history and poetry, truth and verisimilitude, selection of the important events and exclusion of the others, and so on, as they appear in part I. Cide Hamete is criticized for having included two extraneous narratives: the captive captain's story of his adventures and escape from Algiers (I:39–43) and the written novella called "A Story of Ill-advised Curiosity" (I:33–35). In chapter 44 Cide Hamete will have an opportunity to respond to these criticisms and to describe the new technique he has chosen to employ in part II. Here at the beginning the characters discuss the wisdom of sequels in general (can the continuation ever be as good as the original?), and the purity of the writer's motives (is he just trying to cash in on the success of the first part, or does he have something new to say?).

Before they set out on the third sally, Don Quixote and Sancho are brought together and the necessity of their relationship is insisted upon in various ways (II:1–7). The priest observes, for example, that "it seems as though they had both been cast in the same mold, and the madness of the master without the foolishness of the servant would not be worth a farthing." Don Quixote considers them both members of the same body. Sancho talks to his wife as Don Quixote had formerly talked to him, correcting her grammar and vocabulary and generally demonstrating his cultural superiority. At the same time, the relationship is immediately placed in jeopardy by Sancho, who demands a salary. Don Quixote forces him to choose, pointing out that Sansón Carrasco has offered to serve as his squire, and thereby suggesting that he doesn't need Sancho. Sancho chooses his relationship with Don Quixote over the salary, now claiming that his wife had made him ask for it. Their relationship will be an important theme in part II. It will be threatened by their respective relationships to the socioeconomic order and by their respective relationships to Dulcinea. Don Quixote champions the personalism of feudalism, with its reciprocal sets of mutual obligations, while Sancho wants some kind of capitalism, or at least a relationship based on and mediated by money. Dulcinea herself, or more properly the myth of Dulcinea, is also subject to repeated threats in part II. Don Quixote comes to realize that his own existence depends on the preservation of this myth, yet there comes a time when he will have to choose between Dulcinea and Sancho.

In part I Don Quixote himself created in his mind the world he needed in order to be a knight errant, through a variety of unconscious operations imposed by his madness. In part II he loses control over his own creation, over both the world appropriate to a knight-errant (castles instead of inns, giants instead of windmills) and over Dulcinea.

Other people now present him with real castles, with real knights-errant to challenge him to battle, and what is worse, with a Dulcinea who is not the product of his own desire and his own imagination. The first inkling of this dangerous tendency is Don Quixote's willingness to let Sansón Carrasco write some verses to Dulcinea in his place. This behavior contrasts sharply with his insistence on writing to her himself in I:25. Later, Don Quixote's Dulcinea is replaced by Sancho's (enchanted) Dulcinea (II:10), who is in turn superseded by the duke and duchess's ("real") enchanted Dulcinea (II:30). Over time, this has disastrous effects on Don Quixote's ability to engender the things he needs to keep him alive.

Finally, *Don Quixote II* is full of characters who attempt to stage-manage reality, to turn life into a kind of semi-improvisational theater in which episodes are arranged in order to produce a certain outcome. Sancho's enchantment of Dulcinea (II:10), Sansón Carrasco's impersonation of a knight-errant (II:14) are examples. But in every case, the best-laid plans have a way of going astray, and life asserts itself in its unpredictable spontaneity. This process, which might be thought of as the dialectic of Art and Life, is a fundamental structuring element in *Don Quixote II*. Ciriaco Morón calls it *"el burlador burlado"* (the trickster tricked) and notes perceptively that it extends to the reader, who thinks he's simply going to get more of what made him laugh in part I.

THE THIRD SALLY: II:8–74

The third sally begins by taking up the Dulcinea question with a trip to El Toboso to visit her. This re-creates all the problems that were so neatly averted back in I:32 when Don Quixote's prior commitment prevented him from answering Dulcinea's "summons." Sancho understands that if they actually go to El Toboso and start looking for her he will be caught in his lie, and at some level Don Quixote too seems to understand that to push this search to the limit would be to confront the unreality of Dulcinea. For their separate reasons, both Don Quixote and Sancho come to realize that this mission must be aborted, but that the myth of Dulcinea must be preserved. They reach an unspoken agreement, which Sancho proceeds to subvert. All he needs to do is pretend to have visited Dulcinea, as he did before, and bring his master a message from her to the effect that she doesn't want to see him, and the two of them can leave El Toboso with the problem behind them. Don Quixote even coaches him on what to say, so that his narration of this second imaginary visit to Dulcinea won't be as hard to believe as the first one was. Don Quixote and Sancho are thus the first characters who attempt to stage-manage reality, to control events by turning life into a form of theater. But Sancho decides not to follow the script. He decides he can make Don Quixote believe that any woman—the first one he sees—is Dulcinea. He bases this decision on his massive experience with his master in part I. He knows Don Quixote regularly takes windmills for giants and inns for castles. Unfortunately, he has not understood that Don Quixote's mistakes are the result of inner needs, and he mistakenly believes that they can be induced from without. With this in mind, he identifies three coarse farm girls he spies coming down the road as Dulcinea and her maidens in waiting. Because he has not engendered this identification himself, Don Quixote can see only three coarse farm girls. Try as he might (and he is trying mightily, because belief in Dulcinea is absolutely imperative), he cannot see the beauty Sancho is describing to him. In order to be able to believe in Dulcinea, Don Quixote falls back on his customary explanation: the same enchanter who took his books in I:6 has changed Dulcinea's appearance in order to spite him. She is Dulcinea, all right, but Dulcinea has been enchanted. Sancho has seized control of creation of the myth of Dulcinea. Don Quixote has no choice but to accept this new version of her, no longer his creation but Sancho's. From now on the business of dis-enchanting Dulcinea will be Don Quixote's top priority and will motivate most of the action.

Don Quixote and Sancho now head northeast, toward the city of Zaragoza, where Don Quixote expects to participate in the knightly tournaments in honor of St. George. There is a series of encounters with various people, among them Sansón Carrasco disguised as a knight-errant (II:14–15). He overtakes Don Quixote and Sancho in the woods at night, and when dawn comes we see that his armor is covered with tiny mirrors. He is thus a literal mirror image of our hero, who sees himself reflected in the newcomer's outfit. There is no need for Don Quixote to invent a fantasy, to mentally transform a prosaic reality into an episode from a romance of chivalry, as he did, for example, in I:8 when he took a Basque gentleman for a knight-errant. Sansón is the second character who attempts to turn life into art. He stages a little production featuring himself and Don Quixote in the roles of two knights-errant, in which the older one is defeated by the younger one and sent home to recuperate. The theatrical production is part of a program of therapy, but it backfires. Sansón ought to be able to defeat an old duffer like Don Quixote, but for some reason his horse fails him and Don Quixote wins on a fluke. The therapeutic intent is then replaced by a very real desire for vengeance. It turns out to be impossible not only to stage-manage events, but to remain aloof from them. As the reader is warned in the prologue to part I, it is impossible to remain unaffected, outside, uncommitted. This is what Sansón's attempt at therapy has taught him.

In chapter 16 Don Quixote meets a country hidalgo named Don Diego de Miranda. Don Diego belongs to the same social class as he does, although he is somewhat wealthier. He is a decadent and idle seventeenth-century version of that class, which in the sixteenth century had conquered America and assured Spanish hegemony in Europe by force of arms. In addition, he has a normal family life and he is demonstrably not crazy. He is perfectly integrated into his society. His identity is a function of his lineage, and his life is given over to a round of generally pleasant and socially useful activities. He does not serve his king by engaging in combat. He hunts like a peasant instead of the aristocrat he is supposed to be, and he never reads romances of chivalry. In fact, he is everything Don Quixote presumably ought to be but cannot be. Like Sansón Carrasco in disguise, Don Diego is a kind of mirror image of Don Quixote. He is clearly supposed to be some kind of role model for our hero; the question is whether he is positive or negative. The repeated, insistent contrasting of the two hildagos sug-

gests that although Don Diego fulfills society's expectations and Don
Quixote does not, Don Quixote appears as morally superior. Don
Diego is in fact the first in a series of characters here in part II who
incarnate social roles that in the sixteenth century had been active and
positive, but that had become degenerate parodies of themselves by
1615. While Don Quixote is a guest in Don Diego's house an attempt
is made to ascertain the nature and the limits of his madness, if indeed
he is mad at all. Don Diego and his son both observe that Don Quixote
slips through their fingers, that he defies definition. The best they can
do is something like "an intermittent madman, full of lucid intervals."

On their way again, Don Quixote and Sancho stumble into a
sumptuous country wedding celebration that involves a kind of reprise
of Grisóstomo's suicide in I:14. Because this is part II, however, and
because things are very different here, the disdained lover only pretends to commit suicide, and this allows him to get the girl. A char
acter our heroes meet at these festivities agrees to guide them to the
famous Cave of Montesinos. He is called simply "the cousin," and he
belongs in a series with Don Diego de Miranda. As Don Diego represents the decadence of the hidalgo class, so the cousin represents the
decline into absurdity of humanistic scholarship.

Don Quixote's adventures at the Cave of Montesinos (II:22–23)
are of crucial importance. Lowered by his companions into the cave on
a rope, he falls asleep and has a strange dream. It has been variously
interpreted as a parody of the prophetic dreams of classical epics and
the allegorical dreams of medieval tradition, as an encounter with the
inconsistencies of chivalric romance, as a kind of initiation rite, or
simply as the result of breathing some kind of noxious gas in the cave.
It is also Don Quixote's coming to terms with the new, enchanted
Dulcinea created by Sancho. The dream is inhabited by the farm girls
from II:10, whom Don Quixote now accepts as Dulcinea and her
maidens. This suggests that Sancho's Dulcinea has percolated down to
his unconscious, that he now believes in her as Sancho had hoped he
would immediately in II:10. This also means that Don Quixote has at
least partially regained control of the creation of the myth of Dulcinea
from Sancho.

The brief sojourn at Don Diego's prefigures a much longer stay at the castle (a real castle) of a decadent duke and his duchess somewhere in Aragón. These two sojourns in turn re-create the two visits to Palomeque's inn in part I (I:16–17, 32–46). Here Don Quixote is subjected to a series of humiliating and debilitating experiences organized by the frivolous aristocrats for their own amusement (II:30–57). The duke and duchess are particularly attentive readers of *Don Quixote I*, and they organize their sometimes vicious practical jokes on the basis of their extensive knowledge of part I. One of their most elaborate pranks, the episode of the Countess Trifaldi that culminates in the ride on the "flying horse" Clavileño (II:38–41), is obviously a grandiose elaboration of the Princess Micomicona adventure of I:30, 37. The duke and duchess also appreciated our hero's infatuation with Palomeque's daughter (I:16), and they also perceived his paradoxical combination of strong erotic drives and equally strong terror of women. What could be more natural, then, than to instruct a young lady-in-waiting named Altisidora to pretend to fall in love with him and put him on the spot, with his desire exposed and his chastity at risk? But things are not so simple. Altisidora appears actually to fall in love with him. At the very least, she is truly offended and hurt when he announces he would rather be true to Dulcinea than have a fling with her. She follows the same path already walked by Sansón Carrasco: what begins as fun, an effort to turn life into a form of theater, ends by involving the playactors in something deadly serious. Not only Altisidora, but a *dueña* named Doña Rodríguez becomes seriously involved with Don Quixote. Because the duke and duchess and all their servants make a great show of taking Don Quixote seriously and treating him as a real knight errant, Doña Rodríguez comes to believe that he really is one, and asks him to be her champion in a real case of honor which involves her daughter and one of the duke's vassals. The duke, too, is finally drawn into the affair. He is forced to accept Don Quixote's challenge and, for a moment, to act the part of the aristocrat he is supposed to be, by agreeing to administer justice in his domains.

Again building on his knowledge of part I, the duke fulfills Sancho's dream by awarding him the governorship of an *ínsula,* called

What Happens in Don Quixote II (1615)?

Barataria. Of course it is not an island, but a village on the duke's vast estates, but Sancho doesn't know what an *insula* is anyway. The idea is to place the illiterate bumpkin in a situation beyond his intellectual capabilities, to see what uproarious mistakes he will make. Sancho takes his assignment seriously, however, and proves to be a better ruler than the duke himself. Once again, playacting has strange consequences. In the course of discharging his duties, Sancho decides it's more important to be with Don Quixote than to be a governor (II:45–53). He finally resigns his post and rejoins his master at the ducal palace.

As readers of part I, the duke and duchess know how important Dulcinea is to Don Quixote. They also know she is a figment of his imagination, a myth. With this in mind, they invite him to describe her physically, knowing that he cannot do so. They also ask a number of embarrassing questions about her lineage. They put Don Quixote in a difficult situation for their own amusement, simply in order to see if he can manage to wriggle out of it with the myth of Dulcinea intact. They know too that Sancho failed to deliver his master's letter to her in part I, and that his narration in I:31 was a lie. They can expose Sancho in his lie if they choose, and they can destroy the myth of Dulcinea by increasing the pressure on Don Quixote to discuss her. When they learn that Dulcinea has been "enchanted" as a consequence of the trip to El Toboso in II:10, they rise to new heights of gratuitous cruelty. The duchess in particular plays with Sancho's painfully obvious desire to be in her good graces. When he tries to ingratiate himself with her by telling her he had made up the enchantment, she retorts that he is mistaken, that in fact Dulcinea really is enchanted. What can he do? The aristocrats wrest control of the myth of Dulcinea away from Sancho and institute an adversarial relationship between him and Don Quixote that threatens to tear them asunder. They mount a truly spectacular production, featuring appearances by the enchanted Dulcinea herself (played by a comely young page boy) and Merlin the Magician, who decrees that the key to her disenchantment shall be 3,300 self-inflicted lashes to Sancho's own ample posterior (II:33). Even this detail reveals the duke and duchess's careful reading of part

I. Sancho's "ample posterior" is explicitly mentioned in the nocturnal adventure of I:20, and his aversion to physical pain is well established generally. Sancho refuses to participate, whereupon the duke provides an incentive by informing him that unless he does, there will be no governorship. The duke and duchess have succeeded in polarizing Sancho and Don Quixote by making what each of them holds most dear depend on the other. This creates an antagonism that persists almost until the end of the book. From now on the relationship will be haunted by what we might call the "whiplash factor," Sancho ingeniously trying to evade what Don Quixote most wants him to do, provoking crisis after crisis.

In the midst of Don Quixote's misadventures at the ducal palace, Cide Hamete Benengeli comes forward in II:44 to answer criticisms of his narrative procedures in part I, and to describe the new system he had adopted here in part II. The seminar on narrative theory and practice is open again. What is at issue is the interpolated stories of part I, especially the captive captain's narration and "A Story of Ill-advised Curiosity." This time he says he will limit himself to a few "episodes arising out of the circumstances the facts present."

After he takes his leave of the duke and duchess, Don Quixote discovers the existence of the inauthentic second part by Avellaneda (II:59). When the two readers of Avellaneda's book meet Don Quixote and Sancho they immediately perceive the difference between them and the imitation versions. Later on (II:72) our hero meets a character from Avellaneda's book, a certain Don Alvaro Tarfe, who is only too pleased to sign a notarized document stating that there is no resemblance between the two Don Quixotes. The phony one had fallen out of love with Dulcinea and had attended the jousts in Zaragoza as announced at the end of part I. In order to demonstrate the other's inauthenticity, our hero reaffirms his undying love for Dulcinea and decides to go not to Zaragoza but instead to Barcelona.

On the road he meets the Catalan bandit Roque Guinart, a kind of decadent, seventeenth-century version of the ideals of chivalry. Roque is another in the series of degenerate modern versions of ideals that had ceased to be functional. On the beach in Barcelona Don

What Happens in Don Quixote II *(1615)?*

Quixote is overtaken by Sansón Carrasco, disguised again as a knight-errant in full armor (II:64). This Knight of the White Moon challenges our hero to single combat on the grounds that his lady, "whoever she may be," is more beautiful than Dulcinea, and this time defeats him easily. At the apex of his heroism, lying on the ground with the other knight's lance at his throat, his voice echoing around inside his helmet "as though coming from a tomb," Don Quixote reaffirms Dulcinea's peerless beauty and pleads to be killed because he has failed to defend it adequately. This episode provides the measure of just how much Dulcinea has come to mean to him. She is dearer to him than life itself, or phrased another way, she is his life. Instead of killing him, however, Sansón extracts from him a promise to return home and refrain from the exercise of knight-errantry for a year.

On the way home he decides to convert his year of forced retirement into a kind of sabbatical where he and Sancho will be literary shepherds instead of chivalric characters, and where the myth of Dulcinea can continue uninterrupted (II:67). Being "the one who is in love with Dulcinea" turns out to be more important to our hero than being a knight-errant. On the way back to La Mancha the antagonism between Don Quixote and Sancho over Dulcinea's dis-enchantment comes to a head. Every other means of persuasion having failed, Don Quixote agrees to pay Sancho a wage for his self-inflicted punishment. Sancho cheats (he beats the trees) but Don Quixote believes he is laying on with such good will that his life is in danger. At this point he has to choose between his love for Dulcinea, with everything that that implies, and his love for Sancho, which is the product of having shared his life for some 120 chapters (II:70). He chooses Sancho, who nevertheless continues to whip the surrounding vegetation until the magic number has been reached and the dis-enchantment effected. This immediately re-creates the crisis (is Dulcinea real? can her reality be put to the test?) that was avoided back in II:10 when Sancho enchanted Dulcinea and put her safely on ice. The fact is that she is a myth, and continued belief in her demands continued effort and acts of will, but Don Quixote is not as strong as he once was, nor is his imagination as active. He has been abused by the duke and duchess. He has been defeated by the Knight of the White Moon. And because he has not been forced to generate imaginatively the kind of circumstance he needs in order to be Don Quixote, and because others have taken over the creation of Dulcinea, his imaginative faculty has grown flabby and is no longer equal to the task of generating a Dulcinea in whom he can believe. He abandons himself to a series of gloomy predictions to the effect that he will never see her as he and Sancho arrive at their village (II:72).

Inside his house he is greeted by his niece and housekeeper. The former ridicules his advanced age and weakness, and the latter counsels him to adopt the deadeningly conformist life-style typified by Don Diego de Miranda. Don Quixote throws in the towel. He goes to bed, and when he wakes up he abandons his existence as Don Quixote in order to assume a new one, that of Alonso Quijano el Bueno, for the purpose of dying an exemplary Christian death (II:74). The novel ends with Don Quixote gone and Alonso Quijano dead and buried. Cide Hamete Benengeli's pen has the final word, insisting on the authenticity of his characters and on the impossibility of any further continuations.

6

A Book about Books

No book owes so much to preexisting literature, and no book is so different from that literature, as *Don Quixote*. And no author is as conscious of literary tradition and his relation to it as Cervantes. Everyone knows, and Cervantes tells us in his prologue to the first part, that *Don Quixote* was written as an antidote to the romances of chivalry, morally pernicious and without literary merit in spite of their great popularity. We should also observe that in fact the *Quixote* simultaneously incorporates into itself and carries on a dialogue with all the forms of imaginative literature current in late sixteenth-century Spain. It is a book made out of other books and it is a book about books. The massive presence of literature is complemented by a series of theoretical discussions of literature. As we have already seen, the text is simultaneously the story of Don Quixote and his adventures, and the story of its own creation and response to criticism. Many of the characters are avid readers; the course of their lives is determined or altered by their experience with literature. No one, not even illiterate Sancho, remains untouched by books.

Obviously, the predominant form of literature that concerns our text is the chivalric tradition in general. The word *chivalry* derives from French *cheval* (horse), the sign of membership in the aristocratic class, and refers to a model or code of aristocratic ideals and behavior. The literature of chivalry reflects the code, that is, the dominant ideology of medieval Europe: division of society into aristocrats and commoners; feudal organization of the aristocratic hierarchy; emphasis on the values of bravery and skill at arms, loyalty to one's lord, and loyalty also to one's lady fair. The lady frequently was not one's wife, so that loyalty to her also implied the preservation of a secret. The episodes that comprise chivalric literature are generally of two kinds: violent and bloody battles ranging from individual encounters between two knights to pitched battles involving thousands, and amorous interludes featuring the knights and their ladies. This literature is also populated by a number of wizards, sorcerers, enchanters, and others of both sexes who have access to supernatural power. They can alter appearance so that people seem to be transformed into others, they can render people and objects invisible, they can transport people over great distances with incredible speed, and so on. In other words, although the literature of chivalry reflects the structure and values of feudal society, it also has a marked bias toward fantasy, unreality, and wish fulfillment through magic. The stories of knights-errant and their ladies formed a vast body of material that existed all over Western Europe in a number of different forms, with differing ideological orientations emerging over time.

We English speakers are most familiar with the Arthurian cycle of chivalric romance, the adventures of King Arthur and the Knights of the Round Table. This material finds its way into *Don Quixote,* but far and away the most pervasive manifestation of the chivalric tradition in the *Quixote* is constituted by the Spanish romances of chivalry. Probably the closest analogue that we have today to the ethos and appeal of those old books would be the James Bond films, a series that has continued after the death of Bond's creator and which has now employed three or four different actors in the role of Bond. Bond is a typical hero of romance: just a shade larger than life, physically invincible, irresistible to women, and always on the side of right as that is defined by the dominant ideology. He moves from one exotic and glamorous locale to another, he is surrounded by a wealth of high-tech gadgetry, he is always impeccably dressed, he always wins at cards and roulette, and he never has the slightest doubt about who he is, what he believes, or why he does what he does. In fact, he has no interior dimension at all. His character does not evolve as he accumulates experience and reacts to it. This is the essence of the romance genre, perhaps its most fundamental and profound difference from the novel. Each new Bond film offers us more of the same, although the locales may change and the antagonists may vary superficially. One of the appeals of these films, in fact, is their comforting repetitiousness. This characteristic calls to mind another contemporary analogue, although not as precise, of the old Spanish romances of chivalry. These are the Rocky and the Rambo films, with their theoretically interminable sequels.

The Spanish knights-errant not only appeared in various adventures themselves; they had sons and nephews who succeeded them and became the heroes of new books. The Spanish romances of chivalry are in fact organized into a series of dynasties. Of these, far and away the most important is that of Amadís de Gaula and his progeny. Amadís is the paradigmatic figure of the genre, a superhero who accomplishes super deeds. He is the bravest, the strongest, the most loyal to his sovereign and to his lady. This last characteristic introduces a fundamental difference between the old romances and their modern counterparts. Bond's casual promiscuity would have been unacceptable to Amadís and almost all of his contemporaries, who took the chivalric ideal of loyalty to one's lady very seriously. The first four books of the Amadís cycle, entitled *Amadís de Gaula*, were published together in 1508 by Garci Rodríguez de Montalvo. Book 5 is devoted to the exploits of Amadís's son Esplandián. Book 6 is about Florisando, the son of Amadís's brother Florestán. Book 6 and 7 deal with Esplandián's son, Lisuarte of Greece, whose son Amadís of Greece is the hero of book 9, and so on for another three books.

Like the Bond and the Rambo films and their like, these books were enormously popular and influential. It would be inappropriate for us to sneer at them from our academic ivory tower. They offer the possibility of numberless sequels not because they are bad art, but because they appeal so powerfully to basic instincts within us. And they can move us to action. Ignatius Loyola's reading of romances of chivalry while convalescing from a wound is said to have resulted in the creation of the Society of Jesus. The religious order was to be modeled on the order of knighthood, working actively and strenuously in the world "for the greater glory of God." Teresa of Avila read the romances when she was a little girl and determined to emulate their heroes by going off with her brother in search of violence and death in the cause of Christianity. The militant spirit of the Counter-Reformation in general is traceable at least in part to the pervasiveness of these books in Spanish society. The Spaniards who explored and subjugated the New World had a sense of actually living out a gigantic romance of chivalry. When Cortés and his men came to the Aztec capital of Tenochtitlán they had never seen anything like it. In order to describe it, the chronicler Bernal Díaz del Castillo falls back on the description of an enchanted city from one of the books. When the Spaniards reached what seemed to be an island off the northwest coast of Mexico they named it California, after an island in the Esplandián book ruled by a black Amazon queen named Calafia. With all this going on, is it any wonder that an anonymous country hidalgo should also immerse himself in these books? And is it so unusual that they should exert an influence on his life?

A second great source of Don Quixote's knowledge of chivalry is the much more courtly Italian epic tradition, present chiefly in the works of Matteo Boiardo (1441–94) and Ludovico Ariosto (1474–1533). Both these writers take up the adventures of Roland, renamed in his Italian form, Orlando. Roland is the most important hero of yet a third cycle of chivalric fiction, the Carolingian, which deals with the exploits of King Charlemagne and his knights, the struggles between Christians and Moors in the Pyrenees and southern France. The best known work in this cycle is the eleventh-century *Chanson de Roland* (Song of Roland). Boiardo and Ariosto continue the cycle with Roland-Orlando's further adventures, related in long poems in the style of the classical epic. Boiardo's poem (1495) is called *Orlando innamorato* (Orlando in love). It tells how Orlando was hopelessly smitten by a certain Angelica la Bella and how she keeps eluding him.

Ariosto's 1516 sequel, *Orlando furioso* (Orlando insane), is much more interesting and much more visible in the *Quixote*. Here Angelica falls in love herself, but not with Orlando. She gives herself instead to a teenaged Moor named Medoro. Orlando comes upon the rustic cabin where they have consummated their relationship, finds unmistakable evidence of what has occurred there, and plunges headlong into psychosis. In his insane rage he tears up trees by the roots and does all sorts of other violence. He is finally brought back to sanity by another knight named Astolfo, who flies to the moon on a magical horse, finds Orlando's brains in a glass vial, and returns with them to earth. It will be apparent that Ariosto does not take the chivalric tradition and value system entirely seriously. In fact, his poem begins to parody a life-style and a literary tradition that the Spanish romances of chivalry still respect. Cervantes and his hero are both great readers of Ariosto. The whole idea of a mad protagonist whose life subverts society's norms is immediately referable to him. Within the text, Don Quixote at one point (I:25) decides to imitate specific features of Orlando's madness, and later (II:62) he modestly refers to his ability to sing some of Ariosto's verses.

Chivalric material also finds its way into the *Quixote* through the great body of traditional Spanish ballads. These were the songs everybody knew, that circulated in printed collections but especially in oral form. They furnish chivalric stories especially from the Carolingian and Arthurian store. Don Quixote in particular is obsessed by the story of Lancelot and Guinevere. He embeds a reference to it in the speech he makes as he arrives at the first inn (I:3), casting himself in the role of Lancelot but stopping short of mentioning Guinevere explicitly. In fact there is no need to allude directly to the adulterous affair. When Don Quixote quotes the first few lines of the appropriate ballad, his listeners (and Cervantes's readers) could be counted upon to supply the rest from memory. There is another aspect to the presence of the ballad tradition in the *Quixote*. Just about the time of its publication there appeared an anonymous theatrical piece called *El entremés de los romances* (The one-act play about ballads). Its hero is a peasant named Bartolo who becomes so wrapped up in the world of the ballads that he loses touch with reality and takes on the identities of various ballad characters. Don Quixote also slips into a couple of these roles himself (I:5). It has been suggested that Cervantes's original conception of Don Quixote is derived from this little play. Or someone else may have been inspired by reading Cervantes. Nobody knows, but what is apparent is the pervasiveness and the immediate availability of the ballad tradition for incorporation into other genres.

Clearly, Don Quixote as a person and the *Quixote* as a text would be impossible without the literature of chivalry, but it also incorporates every other tradition current in Cervantes's time. The most important of these is probably the pastoral. Pastoral literature has an impeccable pedigree but a bad press. It was cultivated by the foremost poets of antiquity, especially Virgil and Horace, and it was rediscovered and revived as a highbrow genre in the Renaissance. We have a hard time relating to it because it seems hopelessly artificial. Shepherds who sound more like philosophers sit around under the trees and talk endlessly, and in verse, about love. This is escapist literature, but it is an escape from the distractions of life to a confrontation with oneself and one's most intimate feelings. It is thus very serious, in spite of its apparent divorce from reality. In 1559 Jorge de Montemayor published a book-length work of prose fiction called *La Diana,* which combines the lyrical introspection typical of the pastoral tradition with the action of narrative, and a new genre, the pastoral romance, was born. There was a vogue for these pastoral romances (as there was for the chivalric romances) throughout the remainder of the sixteenth century. In fact, Cervantes's first work of prose fiction is a pastoral romance called *La Galatea* (1585). Just as chivalric romance offers an anonymous hidalgo a way out of his impossible situation at home and the hope of a new life as Don Quixote, so pastoral romance offers Marcela exactly the same kind of opportunity in I:12–14. She retreats from an intolerable situation, besieged by every young man in the county, into the existence of a literary shepherdess, free to sit under the trees and talk endlessly about love without ever having to commit herself or choose a husband. In I:52 two male characters, Eugenio and Anselmo, also retreat into the pattern of existence offered by pastoral literature at the conclusion of a tragic love affair. They transmute the pain of experience into art as literary shepherds have always done, tending their sheep and singing under the trees. In part II the situation is more complex. In II:58 we meet some fairly shallow young people who are out in the country playing at being literary shepherds, complete with recitations of pastoral poems by famous poets. Their exercise trivializes the possibility of pastoral literature as a refuge from the intolerable demands of life seized on by the characters in part I, but Don Quixote makes it real and vital again. After his defeat by the Knight of the White Moon in II:64 he is to abstain from the practice of chivalry for a year. It occurs to him to fill the time by trading his chivalric life-style for a pastoral one, also derived from literature. What authenticates this exercise and allows our hero to be true to himself is the continued presence of Dulcinea as the object of his affections. He will (temporarily) change his name from Don Quixote to "the shepherd Quixotiz," but his identity will continue to be "the one who depends for his existence on Dulcinea."

The Spanish picaresque tradition is a third major literary presence in *Don Quixote*. Paradoxically, what is noted in the text is its absence, the fact that *Don Quixote* is an antipicaresque book. This genre was initiated by the anonymous *Lazarillo de Tormes* (1554) and consolidated by Mateo Alemán's *Guzmán de Alfarache* (1599 and 1604). We should observe in passing that *Guzmán,* not *Don Quixote,* was the most popular work of fiction in the early seventeenth century, both in Spain and elsewhere in Europe. The picaresque books recount the adventures of a rogue who tries with greater or lesser success to integrate himself and rise in respectable society. They generally take the form of fictional autobiographies of criminals. In I:22 we meet such a criminal, the condemned galley slave Ginés de Pasamonte, who furthermore is writing his autobiography, which he furthermore compares to the fictional *Lazarillo* and *Guzmán.* Ginés bears a strange resemblance to Guzmán de Alfarache himself, who is supposed to have written his autobiography while condemned to the galleys. Don Quixote is immediately sympathetic to Ginés because he senses that his life, like his own, is inextricably bound up with literature. When asked if his book is finished Ginés responds: "How can it be, when my life is not finished yet?" Ginés's comment certainly suggests that literature and life are intertwined and coterminous, but it also points to something Cervantes considered a fatal flaw in the narrative strategy and resulting vision of the world possible in the picaresque format. Ginés, like Lazarillo and Guzmán, is the only speaker in his text. Consequently, everything that appears there can be presented from only one point of view, having been filtered through only one particular consciousness. There is no opportunity for that interplay of multiple authorial perspectives and differing value judgments that is the hallmark of Cervantes's works. More prosaic, but no less a problem, is the fact that the autobiographical format of the picaresque prevents the narration of the end of the story. No protagonist, not even the multitalented Ginés de Pasamonte, can narrate his own death.

Cervantes as a writer presents the picaresque format embodied in Ginés de Pasamonte only to reject it. Don Quixote as a character who willfully patterns his life on the models provided by literature also rejects the picaresque as it is offered in I:14. At the conclusion of the Marcela-Grisóstomo affair some travelers invite him to accompany them to Sevilla, which they remark is a place where adventure lurks around every corner. Don Quixote declines their invitation, on the grounds that much knightly work remains to be done in La Mancha. The real reason is left unstated. If he were to go to Sevilla and engage in the kind of adventures the big city offers, his life would cease to be a romance of chivalry and become instead a picaresque book, and he in turn would become something or somebody different from what he has set out to become. He needs to remain out in the country in order to be Don Quixote.

A final genre, also present as a possibility not acted upon, is the so-called Byzantine romance. This genre originated in antiquity and consisted basically of two texts: Heliodorus' *Aethiopic History of the Loves of Theagenes and Chariclea* (third century B.C.) and Achilles Tatius's *History of the Loves of Leucippe and Clitophon* (third century A.D.). Like the pastoral, the Byzantine genre was revived and imitated as a highbrow form in the Renaissance. Guardians of literary taste and public morals prized the Byzantine romances and opposed them to the nefarious romances of chivalry, holding them up as models to be imitated. They were everything the romances of chivalry were not. Derived from the classical epic of Homer and Virgil, these books presented the adventures of a pair of separated but faithful lovers who manage to preserve their chastity from a variety of attacks in a variety of geographical settings. They offered their readers lessons in real geography, as opposed to the fanciful versions in the chivalric books. They offered positive moral lessons, chastity until faithful marriage instead of chivalry's clandestine pre- and extramarital trysts. There are no magical episodes to strain the reader's credulity. These books offered plots with logical connections of cause and effect, as well as a sophisticated narrative technique borrowed from the epic, considered the highest form of literary expression. They embodied all the features of good literature presented in Aristotle's *Poetics* and, as one critic has remarked only half in jest, they were even written in Greek. They offered the serious modern writer a model for a new kind of prose fiction based on the Aristotelian precepts, and their existence demonstrated that the epic could be written in prose, as well as in verse. In spite of, or perhaps because of all these markers of cultural status, the Byzantine romances never began to approach the popularity of the artistically inferior, morally suspect romances of chivalry. They are present in the *Quixote* only as a possibility, in the discussion between the priest and the canon of Toledo in I:47–48 concerning the romances of chivalry and their defects. There are specific references to Homer and Virgil, to prose epics that would follow Aristotle's precepts, and the like. But *Don Quixote* is nothing like a Byzantine romance. That genre, present here only by reference, is worked out only in Cervantes's last published work, the posthumous *Travails of Persiles and Sigismunda* (1617), a modern Byzantine romance that does indeed embody the themes and artistic precepts so congenial to the priest and the canon. What we have in the *Quixote* is a dialectic of competing literary theories: the Aristotelian poetics of verisimilitude championed by the two ecclesiatics, and the medieval, chivalric poetics of fantasy exemplified in Don Quixote's brief narration in I:50.

We have now come full circle, from chivalric romance to chivalric romance. It should by now be apparent that Cervantes had discovered the art of making literature out of other literature, the phenomenon known in contemporary critical discourse as *intertextuality*. It should also be apparent that *Don Quixote* does not repeat any particular mode of preexisting literature, but rather incorporates and engages them all, subjecting them to Cervantes's own critical examination and making them serve his own purposes. The composition of *Don Quixote* may thus be said to be an exercise in rewriting the older texts. Perhaps his most interesting achievement in this regard is his incorporation into part II of part I of his own creation, as he had incorporated all preexisting literature into part I.

All this literature functions in various ways in Cervantes's text. Perhaps the most obvious, and perhaps the most interesting to contemporary theorists of literary criticism, is the engagement with literary theory itself, the discussions of theory juxtaposed to demonstrations of different aspects of literary practice. Let us consider for example the treatment of Aristotelian literary theory, which was both the last word and the reigning orthodoxy in his time. Aristotle's treatise on literary theory, the *Poetics,* was practically unknown until Giorgio Valla published a Latin translation in 1498. Because it was Aristotle's, it was automatically the most authoritative pronouncement on the subject, and because it had only recently been rediscovered, it was also the last word. Cervantes probably became aware of it through the commentary by his countryman Alonso López Pinciano called *Philosophia antigua poetica* (Ancient philosophy of poetry, 1596). Aristotle divided all writing into two sharply divergent, mutually exclusive categories: history and poetry. History is the record of what actually happened in the world. Its basic criterion is therefore truth. It deals with particular facts as opposed to universal concepts. Poetry, on the other hand, deals with what might plausibly have happened, but didn't. Its basic criterion is not truth, but verisimilitude, the appearance of truth. Poetry deals with issues of universal philosophical or moral import, although it presents them embodied in particular characters and situations.

The text we are reading has been calling itself a history from the beginning, based on archive research and so on. This identification is intensified in I:9 with the introduction of Cide Hamete Benengeli as historian. What Don Quixote and Sancho do is "the truth of the history," a phrase that appears again and again. This "truth" has been ferreted out and recorded by Cide Hamete. But because he is considered unreliable, we have to assume that the "truth" has in all probability been deformed in the very writing of it. This deformed "truth," stated in Arabic, is now translated into Spanish, with the attendant inevitability of inaccuracy. In English we say that "something is lost in the translation." The Italians say it more forcefully in the proverb *traduttore, traditore* (translator, traitor). Finally, the translator's version is subject to revision, deletion, and commentary by the second author, who is the voice who speaks to us. In other words, while repeatedly affirming that this text is true, a history, Cervantes places so many obstacles between the reader and the truth, in the form of this chain of problematic intermediaries, that it becomes impossible for us to know whether what we are reading is true or not. Aristotle's distinction between history and poetry is, at the very least, called into question by this procedure. Cervantes appears to have discovered that once a fact has been passed on from an observer to someone else, and received by that person secondhand, it is impossible to know whether it is really a fact or something the observer/passer-on just made up. Phrased another way, Cervantes discovered that the presence of mediation turns any text into a fiction, and that Aristotle's division is therefore irrelevant.

In addition to blurring the distinction between truth and fiction, the story of Cide Hamete Benengeli and the second author becomes a kind of workshop on the theory and practice of narration. Cide Hamete tells his story, and the second author is free to praise or criticize the Arab's narrative procedures. To make matters more complex, criticism sometimes masquerades as praise. In I:16, for example, we meet a couple of mule drivers at Juan Palomeque's inn. They are described in great detail, much greater detail than necessary, in fact, for such minor characters. The second author praises Cide Hamete for providing such a wealth of information about them. The lavish praise of Cide Hamete is in fact a criticism, ironic, the opposite of what it appears to be. The second author is suggesting that the historian's task, or the task or any narrator, for that matter, is not to tell everything, but to tell what is relevant. This implies selecting from his narration everything that is not pertinent to the point of the story. In this, once again, Aristotle's distinction between history and poetry is not real. The historian is in fact a storyteller, no different in this from the poet.

Aristotelian theory further assumes that the verisimilar fictional text will attempt to disguise itself as reality, to simulate the flow of experience in its attempt to imitate nature. Instead, Cervantes's text perversely calls attention to itself as a text—an artificial, created object divided into chapters and paragraphs that deny the seamless, ceaseless flow of time. Chapter 4 of part I begins with the phrase "La del alba sería cuando . . ." (It was the one belonging to the dawn when . . .). The *what* belonging to the dawn? The expression is meaningless and incomprehensible in the context of chapter 4. Its meaning depends, logically and grammatically, on the last sentence of chapter 3, which contains the antecedent of the feminine singular pronoun *la*. The mysterious "la del alba" turns out to mean "la *hora* del alba" (the *hour* of dawn, i.e., at first light), when Don Quixote left the inn. There is nothing mysterious in the story. There is a mystery in the text, however, consisting in the separation of a pronoun from its antecedent by a chapter heading, complete with number and title. Cervantes makes us aware of how different a text is from real life, where there are no separations into chapters, and how conditioned we are by the experience of reading to make precisely that sort of separation. In order to capture the sense of what is being said, the reader must mentally obliterate the chapter heading and read the two sentences as though they were contiguous. This is difficult to do. So difficult, in fact, that it took the professional literary critics about 350 years to figure out what "*La del alba*" means.

The second author can criticize Cide Hamete all he likes, but poor Cide Hamete can never speak up in his own defense. The workshop on narrative theory thus turns into a lecture. Cervantes attempts to remedy this lack by creating situations within the fiction (Don Quixote and Sancho) that dramatize many of the same problems that concern the metafiction (Cide Hamete and the second author). In I:20, for example, Sancho tells Don Quixote a story about a shepherdess named Torralba and her lover, a shepherd named Lope Ruiz. His narrative bears an uncanny resemblance to the story told by Cide Hamete: repeated insistence on historical truth, a chain of intermediaries, failure to distinguish between the essential and the accessory, and so on. Don Quixote takes the role of the second author, criticizing Sancho's technique and indeed his entire conception of storytelling. But Sancho, unlike Cide Hamete, can respond to Don Quixote's criticisms. He stoutly defends the narrator's prerogative, even his obligation, to tell his story as he must. The workshop is a real workshop. Like everything else in this book, the question of narrative theory and practice finally comes to include the matter of interpersonal relations.

The episode of Marcela and Grisóstomo (I:12–14) convenes another session of the workshop or seminar on narrative theory and practice. Here there is a group of characters and a series of circumstances and events. Marcela's beauty and fortune are administered by her uncle, the local priest. She has many suitors (after both her beauty and her fortune) but she has no desire to marry. Grisóstomo, home from college, falls in love with her. In order to get away from her suitors, she adopts the life-style of a literary shepherdess. Grisóstomo and his friend Ambrosio follow her and adopt the same life-style. Their behavior is soon imitated by all the other suitors. Grisóstomo dies, leaving some papers. All this is told to Don Quixote (and us) by a succession of male narrators who are only partially in command of the facts and who all hate Marcela and hold her responsible for Grisóstomo's death. We are supposed to organize the discourse of these various narrators into the story of what really happened, and we are strongly urged by their rhetoric to identify with Grisóstomo. Once more there are several intermediaries between the reader and "the truth of the story," but this time they are not grouped into a chain with each one dependent on the preceding one. Their accounts are fragmentary, not necessarily contradictory. Cervantes raises here the issue of the narrator or historian's personal involvement in what he is narrating, and the concomitant loss or impossibility of objectivity. Here it is a matter of masculine stereotypes of women's character and motives, offered as objective "truth." When Marcela herself shows up at Grisóstomo's funeral she tells a completely different version of the events leading up to his death and her responsibility for it. Among other things, Cervantes seems to have anticipated some of the central themes of contemporary feminist criticism.

Sancho's second narration, what he tells Don Quixote in I:31 about his trip to El Toboso, deals again with the Aristotelian questions of history and fiction, and it also dramatizes the very contemporary question of the relation between what happened (the story) and the account of what happened (the discourse). Here Cervantes tackles the apparently self-evident truth that a series of events (a story) has to exist before an account of them (a discourse) can exist. The reader knows that Sancho never made it to El Toboso and consequently never saw Dulcinea. Instead of recounting what happened to him there, which is impossible, Sancho makes up a story (generates a discourse) about Dulcinea based on his knowledge of Aldonza Lorenzo and what Aldonza would probably be doing when he arrived and how she would react to Don Quixote's message. Sancho's story is unacceptable to Don Quixote because Aldonza is not Dulcinea. That is, Don Quixote needs a story about a princess, but Sancho is telling him one about a farm girl. Consequently, he rectifies everything Sancho tells him based on Aldonza and changes it into something appropriate for Dulcinea. The corral becomes a palace, the grains of wheat become pearls, and so on. In other words, there is no "truth," no "story" here at all. The fact is that nothing happened. The story (what happened in El Toboso) is generated by the discourse, in contradistinction to what Aristotelian theory presumes to be the case. Sancho's discourse generates a story in Don Quixote's mind, which because he finds it unacceptable, generates an alternate discourse spoken by him and which provides the kind of "story" he needs. Cervantes understood that the "story," or "what happened," or "the truth," is always a mental construct existing in the mind of a narrator, translated into a discourse encoded in some language, and transmitted in that form to a hearer or reader. This person decodes the discourse, which amounts to changing what he hears or reads into a mental construct of his own. Sancho's narration of his adventures in El Toboso demonstrates first that the story need not precede the discourse, but may in fact be called into existence by it. This in turn suggests that once again, it makes no difference whether there was or was not an actual series of events that provoked the narrator's mental construct, that it is not the events but the mental construct that is encoded and sent on its way to be interpreted. Once again, the Aristotelian distinction between the historian and the poet collapses into the category of storyteller.

In the next chapter the seminar on problems of literary theory and practice continues. There is a spirited discussion of the romances of chivalry involving most of those present at Palomeque's inn: the innkeeper himself; his wife, Maritornes; the daughter, Dorotea; the priest; and Sancho. They are all, with the exception of Sancho, readers or hearers of chivalric romance. Their intensely personal reactions, amounting to a vicarious experience of the sex and violence the books purvey, are combatted by the priest on the standard Aristotelian grounds. Palomeque loves the violence. It distracts him temporarily from browbeating his wife and thereby enters her experience as well. Maritornes identifies with the heroines of the erotic episodes. The daughter offers a modified version, appropriate to her virginal status, of the same interests. This mobilizes her mother again as guardian of the girl's chastity. In answer to the priest's insistence on the distinction between history and fiction, Palomeque declares that it doesn't matter, that the fictions are much more entertaining than real history anyway. The priest is powerless to win these people over, as personal involvement proves stronger than any theory, even Aristotle's. Each one of these characters reacts to the romances of chivalry on the basis of who he or she is and what his or her concerns are. The pervasiveness of personal involvement extends even to Sancho, who, overhearing this talk about romances of chivalry being untrue, begins to have doubts about what Don Quixote has been telling him, and even considers leaving him.

The literary seminar does not simply conclude by opposing fiction to history and suggesting that the former is superior in terms of its ability to engage the affects of readers and hearers. Rather, it progresses to consider, or offer for consideration, the possibility of different types of fiction. In the next chapter the negative critique of the romances of chivalry is complemented and counterbalanced by the reading of "A Story of Ill-advised Curiosity," a modern work of fiction based on Aristotelian principles of verisimilitude and offering characters of enormous psychic complexity. It is customary to consider this story as Cervantes's antidote to the artistically inferior romances of chivalry. I am personally not so sure. Toward the end of part I Cervantes offers a kind of reverse mirror image of what we have just seen here. There is a theoretical discussion of the virtues of what we might call Aristotelian fiction, offset this time by Don Quixote's powerful creation of an episode, a text, conceived according to the poetics of fantasy and wish fulfillment typical of the romances of chivalry. Which is better? How do you define "better"?

In II:26 Don Quixote and Sancho meet Ginés de Pasamonte again. He has taken on a new identity, that of Master Pedro the puppeteer, an itinerant showman who makes his living dramatizing material from chivalric literature. The puppet show he presents reconvenes the seminar on literary theory and practice. There is once again a chain of intermediaries between the audience and the "truth of the story." There is a second author who criticizes the procedures of the first author. The audience is free to criticize the second author, and Don Quixote exercises this prerogative with gusto. Both authors (Ginés and the boy who narrates the show for him) respond to criticism, and the text itself turns out to be a collaborative project, modified by the participation of the audience. Many of the usual concerns surface here: our old friends truth and fiction in general; what to narrate and what to leave out; and the narrator's inability to remain neutral to the fate of his characters. In addition, this session of the seminar takes up the very contemporary critical question of the relative authority of the different authorial voices. Ginés struggles with the narrator, who is supposed to be his subordinate, and sees his work changed around by members of the audience.

Part I is present in part II much as *Amadís* and all the other preexisting literature is present in part I, and in the same way, it is subjected to critical inquiry and modification. In II:44 Cide Hamete Benengeli responds to readers' criticisms of part I, principally the presence of "A Story of Ill-advised Curiosity" (I:33–35) and the captive captain's story (I:39–41). This practice, general in Cervantes's time, of inserting unrelated short narratives into book-length works of fiction raises the question of thematic and structural unity. Cide Hamete explains their presence as a way of relieving himself of the tedium of always having to talk about Don Quixote and Sancho, and of demonstrating his own versatility as a storyteller. Alas, his plan backfired. Nobody thought they belonged there, and nobody bothered to read them, so that Cide Hamete's ability to work in several different narrative genres went unperceived. In part II, he announces, he will refrain from any similar interpolated novelettes and offer instead "only episodes . . . arising out of the circumstances the facts present." That is, the kind of thematic material presented in separate narrations in part I will be integrated into the plot of part II. And integrate he does. "A Story of Ill-advised Curiosity" concerns a character who insists on subjecting a premise that must be taken on faith (his wife's faithfulness, as a matter of fact) to an empirical demonstration, with disastrous results for himself and his marriage. As we know, Don Qixote slept through the reading of this story, so its lesson was not available for him to incorporate into his own life. When he sets out for El Toboso in II:8 he is acting out the tale of ill-advised curiosity himself, subjecting to an impossible empirical demonstration a premise that must be taken on faith, namely the existence of Dulcinea. In this way Cervantes has already kept part of Cide Hamete's promise. The captive captain's narrative belongs to the popular genre of "Moors and Christians." Cervantes returns to this material in a much more personal and intensely moving way in part II when Sancho, returning from his very educational experience as governor, meets some German pilgrims on the road (II:54). One of them turns out to be his old friend and neighbor, Ricote the Morisco, sneaking back into Spain in disguise. The reunion of Sancho and Ricote becomes an exploration of the consequences of the expulsion in 1609 of Spanish subjects of Moorish ethnicity on the lives of ordinary individual Spaniards. Like Master Pedro the puppeteer, Cide Hamete finds himself engaged in a dialogue with readers and critics, and his text acquires its form as a result of this multiple involvement.

The presence of literature in the *Quixote* is massive, overwhelming. Let's try to recapitulate. There is first the almost obsessive insistence on literary theory and practice, the commentaries on existing forms and the playing around with Aristotle's ideas. Within the lives of the characters, literature provides a means of coping with the otherwise intolerable pressures of their personal situations. For Don Quixote and Marcela, to mention only the two most obvious cases, literature offers a model for living, a kind of script for life, a way of transforming life into art. Aristotle believes art imitates life; Cervantes suggests life can imitate art. A wonderful example is Don Quixote's creation (I:25) of an episode in his life exactly as a writer creates an episode in fiction, combining his vast readings, his remote and immediate past experience, and the unconscious preoccupations of which he remains unaware. Finally, literature functions in this book as a device in the service of verisimilitude by making the characters seem more real to us, simply because, as readers, we can have the same experience they can, or they can have the same experience we can. They and we can read *Amadís de Gaula* and discuss its content and artistic merit, and they and we share the experience of reading "A Story of Ill-advised Curiosity" at Palomeque's inn. Because we can share this experience with Cervantes's fictional beings, they tend to seem more like us. They and we all seem to exist on the same ontological plane, at a higher level of reality than Anselmo and Camila and Lotario, and the characters in *Amadís*.

7

Readers and Reading

Professors of literature for some reason seem to be loath to admit it, but every course in literature is really a course in reading. At one end of the spectrum is the instructor who "teaches literature," who more or less eloquently tells the students what the text means. Such an instructor is, perhaps unwittingly, really offering his own reading of the text and requiring the students to read the same way he does. At the other end is an instructor who offers a more creative exploration of the multiple possibilities of meaning that depend on different strategies of reading. The problem with this second teacher's method is that before you know it, any and every interpretation can be declared valid and legitimate. This is especially true if the instructor does not want to be seen as a dictator, or as culturally biased against students whose experience is not like his own, and so on. At worst, the class becomes anarchic and the text becomes meaningless. In the best of cases, the emphasis on reading, on ways of being a reader, on possible strategies of reading, comes to the surface and constitutes the overt material of class discussion, displacing the quest for the meaning (or meanings) of the text. In the final analysis, we professors do not "teach literature." If we teach anything, it is something about being a reader.

We observed in the last chapter that *Don Quixote* is a book about books. We can now add that this necessarily implies a book about reading. Let's begin by considering reading within the *Quixote* itself. Everyone reads, everyone assigns meaning to what he reads, and everyone is affected by what he reads. Even the second author confesses to being a compulsive reader who picks up and reads scraps of paper lying in the street. Don Quixote is of course the principal reader. He deploys a certain strategy of reading, losing himself in the text, ignoring the Aristotelian distinction between history and poetry, using his reading as a script for his own life. The mixed results of this strategy comprise the story of his adventures. It is his reading style that defines him as a person. His style of reading is opposed by just about everyone else, especially his friends the priest and the barber, and the erudite canon from Toledo. Palomeque the innkeeper tends to read more or less like Don Quixote does, but he isn't crazy; his daughter and Maritornes read very differently, from the men and also from each other; the duke and duchess are readers particularly sensitive to significant detail; Don Diego de Miranda refuses to read romances of chivalry; and so on. As readers of *Don Quixote,* we ourselves share with the characters the experience of reading certain other texts, such as *Amadís de Guala* and "A Story of Ill-advised Curiosity." But books and written texts are not the only kind of reading matter. Within the text, the entire world presents itself as a text to be read and interpreted.

When we humans confront any reality, we experience an imperious need to make sense of it. We do this by referring whatever it is to some code or signifying system we have already internalized. For example, when English speakers hear a human voice, we consider the sounds and their sequence as though they were being spoken in English, and what we hear either makes sense to us or not. If we understand, it is because we have in fact been listening to English. Understanding occurs, and meaning becomes possible, only when everyone involved, in this case speaker and listener, refer the phenomenon, in this case a sequence of sounds produced by the human voice, to the same code, or signifying system, in this case the English language. Let's move on to a slightly more complex situation. Suppose an Italian tourist in a Mexican restaurant asks for a little *burro* to go with his bread. This man is in trouble. In his language *burro* means "butter," but in the waiter's Spanish it means "donkey." The problem is not that both tourist and waiter cannot conjure up a valid mental image of *burro*. In fact, the problem is precisely that they can, and do. The difficulty arises from the fact that the word, or signifier, occurs in two different signifying systems, and what it means changes according to whether it is referred to Spanish or to Italian. What does *burro* mean? Nothing, by itself. It only acquires meaning as a member of a signifying system. The ability to interpret, or to assign meaning to a word, is above all a matter of knowing the code.

Modern linguistic science has demonstrated that there is no inherent, organic similarity between the word and whatever it stands for, that *burro* can stand just as well for sweet-tasting animal fat as for a particularly unsweet animal, but in Cervantes's time the arbitrary nature of the linguistic sign had not been discovered. In fact, the professional linguists of the sixteenth century assumed an organic relation. Michel Foucault considers that Cervantes had in effect discovered the arbitrary relation of word to thing, that language is related not so much to things as to mental processes, and by so doing ushered in the modern age.

Natural languages are the most obvious examples of codes or signifying systems, but they are not the only ones. We use artificial languages such as Morse code, musical notation, shorthand, and BASIC. We are surrounded by myriad visual signs whose meaning is established by reference to agreed-upon codes. The red light means "stop," the green means "go." But at sea the same red and green lights mean "left" and "right," respectively. Back in port, the red light means something else. Indeed, every aspect of human understanding depends on our "knowing the code." What do cirrus clouds mean, for example, as opposed to cumulus or nimbus? What does it mean to drive an old Chevy instead of a new Mercedes? Interpreting these signs requires extensive knowledge—of natural phenomena like weather, of the capitalist economic system, of social classes and tensions. The entire world presents itself as a giant text to be read, by Don Quixote and by all the rest of us. Moreover, we are all obliged by our status as humans to be constantly engaged in this process of reading the text and interpreting the signs. When Don Quixote encounters the world, therefore, the debate is not really about the essence of the objects in question (what is this?), but rather about their meaning. This in turn implies meaning to whom, and in relation to what code. That is, the famous "mistaken identity" adventures of part I are really not concerned with identity at all. They are more accurately thought of as semiotic (from *semeion,* a Greek word meaning "sign") adventures, involving questions of signification in relation to codes.

In Don Quixote's first sally he is alone with his thoughts as he comes into contact with the signifiers the world offers. He systematically refers each signifier to the code of chivalry he has internalized through his particular strategies of reading. That large building is the castle, the maidens taking their ease by the portal are high-born ladies, his arrival is announced by music, the man in charge is the castellan, and so on. Our enjoyment is derived from the fact that we know Don Quixote is applying the wrong code as he interprets these signifiers. We know this because the narrator has identified himself with us and estranged Don Quixote from us. He provides us with the appropriate code—the prosaic one—to be applied in the interpretation of the same signifiers.

As we know, the situation becomes more complex with the introduction of Sancho. In their first adventure together there are once again two codes present at the interpretation of the signs, and once again our enjoyment depends on the disparity between them, but now they are both present and in direct confrontation within the fiction. Don Quixote has internalized the chivalric code, based on reading and acts of the imagination, including an imaginative projection of himself into the past. Sancho's prosaic code, on the other hand, results from his internalization of his experience of life in the country, the absence of books, and living in the present. The same signifier is referred by two different interpreters to two different codes, and two different meanings are generated. Don Quixote reads "giants," Sancho "windmills." What those objects *are* is of no particular importance, since what they are does not determine the characters' behavior. The important thing is what they *mean:* what they mean to Don Quixote, and what they mean to Sancho, and why. Cervantes demonstrates in this episode that meaning does not inhere in the signifier, but is rather a function of the particular code to which any given individual can (or must) refer it.

We know the "correct," or appropriate code to be applied in the adventure of the giants/windmills, not because we share Sancho's experience of life in the country, but because the narrator has trained us, told us how to read in this situation. In the adventure of the nocturnal religious procession (I:19) we get something different. Here the narrator chooses not to supply the name of the code to which the signifier (strange moving lights) should be referred, preferring instead to report only what Don Quixote and Sancho see and how they react. Deprived of the code, we are thrown into the same confusion as the protagonists. It is suddenly not so easy for us to feel superior to mad Don Quixote and his errant readings of reality. We are forced to experience his madness from a new and more sympathetic perspective, and we suddenly realize the power the narrator has over us, how he can control our experience by manipulating the semiotic process. We come to understand how crucial it is to know the code.

The semiotic questions arising out of Don Quixote's encounter with an anonymous barber on a rainy day in I:21 are more complex, although the episode begins with a deceptively familiar similarity to what we saw in I:8: the same sign read differently by two interpreters. When the signifier—a shiny object on a man's head—first comes into view, Don Quixote refers it to the code of chivalresque literature and identifies it as the magical helmet of Mambrino, from the Italian epic tradition. We have long since been trained by the narrator to reject the chivalric code, so none of us is tempted to accompany Don Quixote in his reading, but we still don't know how to interpret the shiny object. We can see that it is some kind of headgear, though, and it could be a metal helmet. At this point the narrator divulges not only the appropriate code, but also the particular circumstances that govern its applicability to this case: the barber, his brass basin, his new hat, the rain, the basin used to keep the rain off the new hat. But all is not so simple. For one thing, the barber had already changed the meaning of the object in question from "something to catch whiskers and lather" to "head-gear" by inverting it and putting it on his head when the rain began to fall. The object already exists as a signifier in two different codes, like the word *burro* in Spanish and Italian, before Don Quixote ever sees it. It can still be referred to the barbering code as "basin," but it also belongs to the clothing code as "headgear." From "headgear" to "magical headgear" and the code of chivalric literature is only a short step.

Not only is the meaning of the shiny metal object ambiguous; it turns out that there is another signifier that needs to be interpreted. This is the object on the barber's mule's back, and Sancho wants it for his own donkey. It is a saddle, but what kind? In order for Sancho to gain possession of it, it will have to be inserted into the chivalric literature code, as the saddle of a knight's warhorse, so that Don Quixote can authorize him to take it as the spoils of battle, as he himself claims the "helmet." In order for this to happen, Sancho in turn needs to validate Don Quixote's reading of the shiny metal object as Mambrino's helmet. Within the prosaic code of interpretation, this episode means: "A barber abandons his basin and his mule after being attacked by a madman. The madman steals his basin, and his accomplice steals the packsaddle off the mule." Repositioned within the code of chivalric literature, the meaning of this episode is something like: "Don Quixote defeats a knight wearing the fabled helmet of Mambrino and drives him from the field. He claims the helmet as the spoils of battle, and his squire claims the saddle of the defeated knight's warhorse." And this is what happens, at least on the surface. Both readers, Don Quixote and Sancho, are using the same interpretative code or signifying system to read both objects. The difficulty is that Sancho's reading is not entirely sincere. It is not a function of how he really sees reality, but of his relationship with Don Quixote. He cannot agree wholeheartedly when Don Quixote invites him to admire the "helmet." He finds himself remarking that it is a helmet that looks amazingly like a barber's basin, but Don Quixote refuses to pay attention to these minor discrepancies.

The entire business of reading reality, now intertwined with interpersonal relations, comes to a head in I:45, when everyone is gathered at Palomeque's inn and the barber, the former owner of the objects in question, shows up unexpectedly and lays claim to them. Everyone gets into the act, from his own perspective. Don Quixote insists that the helmet is a helmet, but allows that the saddle looks like a mule's packsaddle to him. How can he be so inconsistent? He is interested only in the helmet. He has no use for the saddle, so he doesn't need to refer it to the code of chivalresque literature. Sancho cannot afford to be so single minded, because his claim to the saddle depends on Don Quixote's reading of the basin as helmet. He wants to agree with his master, but at the same time he has to be true to his own perception of reality. The word he coins, *baciyelmo* in Spanish, a combination of "basin" and "helmet," is a compromise formation that reflects the conflict within him between his relation to the objects in question and his relation to Don Quixote. The question of reading reality is thus inextricably linked to the matter of interpersonal relations, and Don Fernando's subsequent excursion into democracy to determine the objects' "true" meaning only confirms it. Now everyone has a chance to vote, not on the basis of how he reads reality, but according to whether or not he knows Don Quixote and is more or less sympathetic to him. The material reality, the essence of the objects, is a matter of indifference to Cervantes. Nor does the objects' essence change from one moment to the next. This is not a magic show. What changes is the relation between the objects and the people who apprehend them, principally the hapless barber, who sees them drift out of his control before his eyes.

Don Fernando's exercise of the democratic process seems to suggest that it doesn't matter how one reads reality, that any reading is as good as any other, and we're back in the anarchical literature class with the meaningless text. We have to remember that Don Fernando is staging an elaborate joke, funny only because it is based on the premise that in fact one reading really isn't as good as another. But as we have seen, Don Quixote is not joking. His reading of reality, like his reading of the romances of chivalry, is absolutely sincere and in deadly earnest. The question now is *why* does Don Quixote read reality the way he does, in light of the code of chivalresque literature, and *why* does Sancho interpret reality through a different, more historical and prosaic code? The answer is that each man reads the way he does because he is who he is, or more accurately, who he has become. The Spanish philosopher José Ortega y Gassett argued that man is that being who has no being, in the sense of a permanent, immutable essence. Instead of an essence, man has a history. Life presents us with choices, each of us chooses one possibility instead of the others available on each occasion. Over time our choices organize themselves into a pattern typical of each of us. Our history, the aggregate of the choices we have made, comes to define our personality. We are what we have become. In literary terms, this is the phenomenon known as "character." In the case of Don Quixote, the process of choosing began long before chapter 1 of part I. During the fifty-odd years of his life that passed before the narration begins, Don Quixote reacted in some way to the stress posed by the developmental crises of adolescence and young manhood. We don't know precisely how because it's not written down, but we might conjecture that he had trouble forming relationships with women. We do know that he decided not to marry, not to live in the city, not to socialize with the other hidalgos in his little village, and so on. More recently he has reacted to massive new environmental pressure by throwing himself into the reading of romances of chivalry, and finally by flight into psychosis, taking on the identity of a knight-errant and attempting to turn his life into a romance of chivalry. Don Quixote reads reality the way he does because he needs to make the romances of chivalry true. He needs to do this because he is psychotic, and he is psychotic because he has chosen to react in certain ways and not others to the pressures life has subjected him to. We shall have much more to say about Don Quixote's psychosis and its etiology. For now we need to observe the close interrelation of the process of choosing, the formation of character, and the style of reading.

Readers and Reading

In addition to reading previously written texts, and reading reality as a kind of supertext, Cervantes presents numerous instances of reading his own text, *Don Quixote I*, within *Don Quixote II*. We have already remarked that society in part II is devided into those who have read part I and those who have not. The first reader of part I we meet is Sansón Carrasco. He does not dwell on his own experience of reading, although we can see that he has formed certain very definite opinions concerning Don Quixote. What he does discuss at some length is the reaction of the reading public at large, and what he reports accords perfectly with what we have just observed about Don Quixote himself as a reader. Everyone reads the way he does because he is who he is. As Sansón says, "opinions differ because people's tastes are not the same. Some swear by the adventure of the windmills . . . , and others by. . . . One praises the description . . . , another that of . . . , while a third says . . . , and a fourth that . . ." (II:3). The experience of different readers is also related to their age. Adolescent readers are not struck by the same things as their elders, old people react differently from the middle-aged, and so on.

Don Quixote's reverse mirror image, Don Diego de Miranda (II:16), is also a reader, but is ignorant of *Don Quixote I*. Nevertheless, like Don Quixote's, his reading is a function of who he is. He has a library of some six dozen books, not inconsiderable in 1615, which he divides first into those written in Spanish and those written in Latin. He then divides his collection into historical, by which he means both history and fiction, and devotional works. He expresses a preference for works of fiction, as long as they're "chastely entertaining" and "charm by their style and attract and interest by the invention they display." Sounds good, but on closer inspection Don Diego's reading habits turn out to be exercises in ostentation and conformity. He mentions books in Latin (the devotional titles) only to remark that he doesn't read them. Why have them at all, then? Perhaps they add some luster to his house and identify him to his friends and neighbors as a serious, right-thinking gentleman, pillar of the community, and so on. Even more revealing is the word he chooses to describe how he reads the books he does read. It turns out he doesn't read at all. Rather, he "leafs through" these volumes, turning the pages without apparently ever becoming engaged with the imaginary world he holds in his hands. In fact, by reading this way he seems to be actively trying to avoid engagement. He is a reader who has managed to thwart Cervantes's attempt to lock him into his reading. But then, he doesn't read Cervantes. Don Diego's library and reading style define him as conformist, superficial, and uneasy with commitment.

Far and away the most perspicacious and interesting readers of *Don Quixote I* in *Don Quixote II* are the duke and duchess. Curiously, they share some strategies of reading with Don Quixote himself. For example, their continual reading of *Don Quixote* is analogous to our hero's obsession for romances of chivalry. They are criticized for this reading by their chaplain, much as Don Quixote is reprimanded by his friend the priest. They too attempt to put their reading into practice, but where Don Quixote lives out chivalric adventures in his own life, the duke and duchess only stage them for their amusement while remaining on the sidelines themselves. This is an important distinction, because it measures the difference between Don Quixote's absolute sincerity and the two aristocrats' self-centered frivolity.

Keeping this fundamental difference in mind, we can go on to observe that the duke and duchess are very careful readers indeed. All the burlesque adventures they organize for Don Quixote are the result of their attentive reading of part I. Sancho's governorship of the "Island of Barataria" (II:32, 45, 47, 49, 51, 53) of course fulfills Don Quixote's promise to him back in I:7. And their masterpiece, the dis-enchantment of Dulcinea (II:35), would be impossible had they not grasped the desperate seriousness of Don Quixote's need for her, and had they not similarly grasped some important facts about Sancho's personality, his needs, likes, and dislikes. The importance of Sancho's "ample posterior" in the dis-enchantment process is derived from the brief but specific mention of that part of the squire's anatomy when he lowers his pants to defecate in I:20. The duke and duchess have a great eye for at least certain kinds of detail.

The strange case of the Countess Trifaldi (II:36–41) is an amplified version of the therapeutic plan dreamed up by the priest, the barber and the beautiful Dorotea in I:29 to get Don Quixote home where he could be attended to. The countess is clearly a Princess Micomicona on a grander scale and with more supporting players, but there is more. The unfeminine beards she and her ladies are afflicted with grow out of the false beard the barber dons in I:27, made, suggestively, from an "oxtail in which the innkeeper used to stick his comb." The idea of men dressed as women is clearly based on the priest's unseemly impersonation of a damsel in distress, outfitted by the innkeeper's wife in the same chapter. Even though the priest is finally relieved of having to play the role of a woman by the timely appearance of Dorotea, the duke and duchess have retained and intensified the motif of transsexuality that was presented only to be abandoned in part I.

Sexuality is of course at the root of Altisidora's attempt to seduce Don Quixote in II:44. The staged episode is clearly derived from I:16, where Don Quixote believes that Maritornes, on her way to a tryst with a mule driver in the same room, is the innkeeper's daughter coming to offer herself to him. It is the duchess who is particularly sensitive to Don Quixote's sexual insecurities. She sees that he is powerfully attracted to women sexually, and at the same time terrified at the thought of actually having to act on his desires. As a reader of I:16, she understood why he invoked his prior commitment to Dulcinea precisely when he believed his chastity was under attack. Because of her reading of I:16, she understands what motivates Don Quixote's refusal of her offer to place several comely maids in his chamber while Sancho is off being governor in II:44. When he finds himself the object of Altisidora's attentions, even Don Quixote sees the connection to I:16, recalling "the lady for whose sake they beat me in the castle of the enchanted Moor."

Like everyone else, the duke and duchess read what they like to read in *Don Quixote I*. Their reading of the first part, as acted out in the second, shows them to be particularly sensitive to certain kinds of issues and certain kinds of details, which we might summarize as lying within the erotic-sadistic-coprophilic sphere.

One particular reader of *Don Quixote I* finds his way into part II in a strangely circular way. His name remains forever unknown, but he signed himself Alonso Fernández de Avellaneda, and his reading of part I resulted in his own part II, published in Tarragona in 1614. Avellaneda must have been scandalized or terrified or both by his reading of Cervantes's text, because his own version is an attempt to undo it by rewriting it to conform to the official ideology. As a reader, he is diametrically opposed to the duke and duchess, who use their great sensitivity to the nuances of Cervantes's text to ferret out Don Quixote's unconfessed hang-ups and force him to live them out in their presence. Far from being scandalized, they revel in Cervantes's presentation of his hero. Avellaneda is shocked and threatened by him. Avellaneda is present in Cervantes's part II only by reference, through two of his readers and one of his characters. In II:59 we meet two readers of part I who are also readers of Avellaneda's part II. Needless to say, they compare Avellaneda very unfavorably to Cervantes, and when they meet Don Quixote and Sancho in the flesh they do not hesitate to affirm the superiority of Cervantes's characters. In this episode Cervantes gives us a dramatization of a reading and the effects of both on the readers. This is probably the most complex evocation in the entire text of the centrality of reading, like the pebble dropped into the center of the pool that produces an ever widening circle of effects.

I would like now to move outside the text and consider some real readers and readings of *Don Quixote,* among them ourselves. As we know, Cervantes challenges each of us in the first words of the prologue to part I when he addresses us as "unengaged reader" and proceeds to demonstrate how, from that moment, none of us can remain neutral. Like those readers evoked within the text, each of us brings to our experience of reading everything that we have become already, along with our more or less acknowledged desires and our more or less clearly formulated projects. Like the readers within the text, each of us comes to define himself or perceive who he is according to the way he reads *Don Quixote.* Actually, this is what happens when we read any text. Cervantes is merely the first writer in Western literature who understood this and made it a theme of his book, and it must be said that the *Quixote* has a strange power to engage and polarize readers.

Avellaneda is only the first of many readers over the years whose experience of reading *Don Quixote* has resulted in the generation of new texts. These texts are always a consequence of who these readers are and of what strategies of reading they deployed in reading Cervantes's book.

We already know about the great tradition of novels in the cervantine manner, from *Tom Jones* to *The World According to Garp*, as well as more specific "imitations" like Graham Greene's *Monsignor Quixote* (1982), an updated and politicized version of Cervantes's story in which the hero is a naive country priest suddenly elevated to monsignor and Sancho is the Communist mayor of their little town. I want to mention two modern texts that are not usually discussed in light of *Don Quixote*. In *Tristana* (1892) the Spanish novelist Benito Pérez Galdós (1843–1919) re-created Don Quixote's family situation with his niece and housekeeper, but instead of a shy bachelor, his Quixote figure is a great ladies' man, a middle-aged don Juan who maintains his young ward in a state of sexual subjugation, and it is she who must withdraw into literature. Some nine years later Miguel de Unamuno created in *El sencillo don Rafael, cazador y tresillista* another Don Quixote type, a shy, middle-aged bachelor obsessed with the notions of fatherhood and especially motherhood, who finds happiness by marrying and impregnating his housekeeper. All these texts are inspired in some way by, and would be impossible without, *Don Quixote*. Each is the result of a particular strategy of reading, deployed as a consequence of the reader's personality, desires, and so on. The last two in particular develop themes barely hinted at but nevertheless present in Cervantes's work, revealing readers at least as sensitive as the duke and duchess to the sexual dimension of Don Quixote's personality, who reinterpret his sexuality in light of their own. Their works tell us simultaneously a lot about them and about the way they read Cervantes, because as we have already observed again and again, we read the way we do because we are who we are.

What is true of novelists and other creative writers is also true of literary critics and professors, except that the texts we produce as a result of our reading are supposed to be scientific analyses. It is a critical commonplace to observe that *Don Quixote* has generated a body of critical commentary staggering not only in its sheer volume, but also in the number of totally incompatible interpretations and mind-boggling contradictions it offers. A reader like Unamuno, for example, comes to Cervantes's text in search of himself, or at least in search of something that he can recognize and incorporate into his own life. Unamuno reads more or less the same way Don Quixote does. The question he asks the text is, What does this mean to me? He identifies with Don Quixote, against society and against what he perceives to be the attitude of Cervantes himself as his creator. Consequently, when at the end of part II Don Quixote renounces his existence as Don Quixote, assumes the identity of Alonso Quijano el Bueno and reincorporates himself into the fabric of society, Unamuno reads it as a tragedy. A reader like Anthony Close, on the other hand, comes at the text from a totally different perspective, convinced that readers since the early nineteenth century had been misreading it by imposing their own (irrelevant) needs and desires upon it. He is concerned, therefore, to discover what the text meant to Cervantes and his contemporaries, to distance it from himself, in other words to deploy a strategy of reading diametrically opposed to Unamuno's. This leads him to identify with what he perceives as Cervantes's attitude, against Don Quixote and his madness. Consequently, he reads the last chapter, and Don Quixote's acceptance of society's norms, as a triumphant return to right thinking. By asking such radically different questions of the text, or to return to some concepts we have already discussed in this chapter, by referring the same signifiers to such radically different interpretative systems or codes, these readers ensure that they will generate radically different "meanings" of the text. As new strategies of reading come to be employed, the meaning of the text will change as a result. If the episode of Marcela and Grisóstomo is read as it traditionally has been, from a masculine perspective, as the male characters in the text in fact read it, then Marcela is a bitch and Grisóstomo is a victim. But suppose we read the same episode through the lens of contemporary feminist criticism, in terms of categories like patriarchal society and women as the object of exchange among men, what does it mean then?

If we return now to our hypothetical literature classes, we can see that a text can have many legitimate meanings. Meaning does not inhere in the text itself, but is a function of the particular relationship that particular readers establish with it, the experience they bring to it, the codes to which they refer it, and the questions they ask it to answer. More importantly, the text of *Don Quixote* allows us to grasp this fundamental truth because it dramatizes the search for meaning carried on by all the characters in various kinds of reading: of literary texts such as *Amadís de Gaula* and *Don Quixote I*, of realities such as lights moving across the darkness and shiny objects on people's heads, of Don Quixote himself and of the phenomenon of madness as signifier, especially in part II. Like the characters themselves, we all read, we assign meaning to what we read, and we are affected by what we read. In fact, because who we are determines how we read, it might be said that as we read the text, the text is simultaneously reading us, in the sense that our reading has the power to coax out of us and make us recognize aspects of ourselves we didn't know were there, and might prefer not to discover. Maybe this is why Don Diego de Miranda only turns the pages.

8

People, Real and Fictional

We saw in the last chapter that the way each person reads is a function of who he is. In this one I am going to demonstrate the truth of that statement by offering a reading of some important aspects of *Don Quixote,* a reading that will say something about my character, in spite of whatever veneer of scientific objectivity I manage to lay over it. This reading considers Don Quixote and the other characters as though they were real people, or better, as verisimilar literary characters, who act like real people act and whose behavior is determined the same way ours is. This means we should say something about reading and, more importantly, about real people. The act of reading always takes place in the present, but we humans live also in the past, through memory, and in the future, through imagination. We are simultaneously who we have already become (our character) and who we are trying to become (our projects and desires). Furthermore, human activity is by no means limited to reading and intellection. We are constantly acting upon, and being acted upon, by our environment: the people, objects, and institutions with which we come into contact. Our characters and our projects are constantly clashing or meshing with everything around us. Finally, there is a dimension to human life that we are not normally aware of.

People, Real and Fictional

Our behavior is always the result simultaneously of conscious decisions based on more or less rational analyses, and of unconscious impulses derived from the unacknowledged residue of the unresolved intrapsychic conflicts of childhood and adolescence.

Suppose for example that I always buy Ford automobiles for myself and my family. If you asked me why, I would reply that Fords are well built and offer good value, and I would sincerely believe this is true. But maybe there is also something else. Maybe I am also moved to buy Fords because my father could never stand Fords, and was always telling me how tinny and unreliable they are. And because, unbeknownst to myself, I am still in an adolescent rebellion against my father, my insistence on buying Fords is really an act of defiance against his authority. The only observable behavior is my purchase of the Ford cars, but it is the result simultaneously of two motivations: a conscious, socially acceptable choice based on advertising and favorable experience, and an unconscious need, which I keep hidden even from myself, to overturn my father's authority. This hidden motivation is in fact more powerful and compelling than the conscious one, but unless there is some trouble, I will live out my life in blissful ignorance of it, congratulating myself on my prudent car buying and adult decision-making.

All human behavior is doubly motivated in this way. We only think we consciously choose one alternative over others, as in the case of buying Fords or some other car, and we also only think we react to environmental stress in a totally rational and conscious way. In fact we constantly mobilize unconscious mechanisms of defense to shield our fragile egos from pressures we would rather not bear. The one we all mobilize most frequently is called repression, a clinical name for forgetting. We forget things that would cause us discomfort if we remembered them. Or we displace feelings for one object onto another, where the discharge of our emotions won't result in intolerable consequences. We yell at our spouse and our children without realizing that we do so because we can't yell at our boss, for instance. There is a whole hierarchy of these unconscious protective devices. Some are techniques we all employ. They may be mildly annoying, but they don't seem strange, or far out, to our friends and associates. These defenses have been characterized as "adult" and "neurotic." Others are more extreme: actually punching out the annoying coworker instead of just wanting to, retreating into a fantasy instead of confronting the situation, getting sick when we feel unloved, attributing our own hostile or otherwise unacceptable impulses to someone else. These are the "immature" defenses. They don't really make life any easier for the person who mobilizes them to deal with stress, and they make other people very uncomfortable. Finally, thre is a group of frankly psychotic defenses. These include Don Quixote's standby of grossly reshaping external reality to conform to inner needs, the denial of reality as it is, and just plain having delusions about the way things are. It is interesting to observe that the immature defenses involve flawed relatons with other people, while the psychotic ones deal with objects and institutions. As we proceed through life, each of us develops a particular "coping style." That is, we tend to mobilize a particular constellation of unconscious defenses that comes to be characteristic of us as individuals, or to define our personalities. The kind of defenses we choose also tends to locate us along the mental health spectrum from the "normal-neurotic." to the "immature-psychotic" or "crazy."

If verisimilar literary characters act like real people, it is reasonable to assume that their behavior, like ours, is doubly motivated, that it is simultaneously the result of conscious choice and unconscious pressure. Aristotle was groping for this when he said that the characters in literature who really get to us, who move us deeply, are "people like ourselves," by which he meant people who act like we do and in whom we can recognize ourselves. The characters Aristotle had in mind are people like King Oedipus, who murders his father and commits incest with his mother. It cannot be in these overt ways that Oedipus is "someone like us." The recognition Aristotle speaks of is generally more effective at the unconscious level of perception than on the surface. It is easy, though trivial, to identify with James Bond, for example, but he really isn't very much like us. We have already observed that Bond has no inner life. But there is something that reaches out and hooks us in Oedipus, even though we aren't incestuous parricides; in Faust, even though we don't sell our souls to the devil; and in Hamlet, Don Juan, Raskolnikov, Emma Bovary, and of course Don Quixote, even though we don's share any of the particular circumstances of their lives. Norman Holland has formulated this process as the reader's unconscious search for what he calls his "identity theme," a complex of issues and responses that constitutes the psychic thematics of the reader's own life and which he recognizes, or senses, in certain characters in fiction. As we read, our own unconscious resonates in harmony, or rejects resonance, with the characters' unconscious. Something in their humanity touches ours, below the level of consciousness. We are quite literally "moved deeply." This is another way of saying, as we did at the end of the last chapter, that as we read the text, the text also reads us.

Let's come to Don Quixote. Why should an anonymous hidalgo suddenly go crazy and ride off into a fantasy world of knights-errant and ladies fair? Is there some real reason, or is his madness unmotivated, merely a pretext to get him on the road so he can interact comically with reality? If Don Quixote is a verisimilar character, his behavior ought to be motivated as ours is, by a combination of publicly verifiable conscious choices and unconscious proddings of which he remains unaware. In the rest of this chapter I want to try to trace Don Quixote's behavior back to its unspoken motivation, beginning with the etiology of his psychosis. We might begin by reviewing what we know about him at the beginning of the novel. He is about fifty years of age, an hidalgo of very modest means slowly being squeezed into poverty by inflation. A bachelor, he lives in a little village somewhere in La Mancha, in the company of his niece not yet twenty, and a housekeeper about his own age.

He is a fifty-year-old bachelor. What does that mean? What do we know about fifty-year-old men in general? We have been hearing a lot in the last ten years or so about something called midlife crisis, or what happens to men around the age of fifty. We are probably all familiar with the bizarre behavior sometimes displayed by men in midlife. Paul Gauguin leaves a good job as a Paris stockbroker and sails off to Tahiti to paint bare-breasted women. A lawyer I know gives up his practice in order to devote himself to an import business specializing in cardboard binoculars and electric T-shirts. An attempt is made to deny the fact of advancing age by engaging in behavior appropriate to much younger men. My colleagues show up for work dressed like undergraduates. Several of them divorce their wives and marry students young enough to be their daughters. From many different scientific perspectives evidence has been accumulating that suggests that midlife is in certain crucial ways a kind of replay of adolescence. Physiologists point to an analogous hormonal imbalance characteristic of both periods in the life cycle. Psychoanalysts observe a resurgence of the Oedipal conflict typical of adolescence. This might be thought of as the struggle to keep suddenly strong, unacceptable sexual and aggressive impulses from becoming too openly and directly expressed. These are the same ones we feel originally toward the parent of the opposite and the same sex, respectively. Normally, these impulses are kept at bay or channeled into socially acceptable activities by a combination of ego defenses, but at certain times in our life there is an upsurge so strong that, in spite of our best efforts, real or fantasized sexual activity results. These times are adolescence and midlife.

If this is the clinical profile of men in midlife, it would seem that Don Quixote is a worthy example. He certainly effects a "midlife career change," not unlike Gauguin and my friend the lawyer, by leaving a settled life-style and becoming a knight-errant. What about the resurgence of adolescent sexual impulses? We should remember here that Don Quixote is a bachelor. That is, he didn't resolve the Oedipal conflict typical of adolescence in the normal way, by transferring his feelings for his mother to an acceptable woman of his own age, courting, marrying, and having a family. And on the basis of his awkwardness around women we can reasonably conjecture that he is also a virgin. This suggests that the particular Oedipal conflict he reexperiences in midlife is unresolved, that he returns to a lifelong conflict between sexual energy and a chronic inability to find sexual outlets for it. It is not merely desire that comes to the fore at age fifty, but desire thwarted and ungratified, possibly from some deep-seated fear of women. Of course the text doesn't tell us any of this. These are the reasonable inferences we can make on the basis of what the text does tell us, namely that Don Quixote is fifty years old and a bachelor.

His life is monotony itself. His status as hidalgo condemns him to inactivity. He has two suits of clothes, one for weekdays and one for Sundays. His diet is the same, fifty-two weeks a year. He has but two friends, who furthermore are not chosen from among his fellow hidalgos. His existence is so unremarkable that we don't even know what his name is. The only thing that distinguishes him, as we know, is his passion for reading romances of chivalry. For a long time nobody really thought to ask why he is such a voracious reader. It was Unamuno who first proposed, in 1905, that he reads as he does in order to take his mind off a certain Aldonza Lorenzo, a farm girl from neighboring El Toboso whom he has worshiped from afar for twelve years, during which time he has actually seen her maybe four times. According to Unamuno, he is still in love with her, but too timid to declare himself and ask for her hand. In 1934 a psychoanalyst named Helene Deutsch repeated the hypothesis, with suitable professional terminology. This is suggestive, because we know that by the end of chapter 1 Aldonza has in fact been transformed into Dulcinea del Toboso. In order to avoid having to admit his impotence to himself, so the thesis goes, Don Quixote gets rid of Aldonza by promoting her to the category of literary princess, a creature by definition unattainable, so that his failure to approach her need no longer bother him. This makes perfect sense, until we ask ourselves why a sensitive, educated man like Don Quixote would fall in love with a loud, coarse, mannish girl like Aldonza in the first place. In I:25 Sancho offers a description of her, which Don Quixote does not contradict, as a girl "with hair on her chest," who drinks and trades jokes with the men down at the local saloon, who has a voice you can hear for miles around, and so on. Not exactly Don Quixote's type, especially if we recall his infatuations with the innkeeper's daughter in part I and with Altisidora in part II.

The inconsistency we have just observed between Aldonza and other objects of Don Quixote's affections invites us to deploy a particular strategy of reading. Most such strategies, especially the ones we tend to hear about in literature classes, strive toward a reading that integrates all the data presented in the text into a meaningful and coherent whole. When I was an undergraduate everyone talked about "organic unity," the idea that everything in a work of art supports everything else in the production of a single meaning. We professors have now absorbed some of the lessons Cervantes teaches us about readers and reading in *Don Quixote,* and in many if not most literature classes today we are prepared to admit a multiplicity of possible legitimate meanings generated by different styles and strategies of reading. For the most part, however, these strategies continue to be based on the notions of unity and consistency, with the result that discrepancies like the one we have just noted tend to be passed over in silence or explained away.

There is another way of reading, one that actually focuses on the anomalies and inconsistencies in the text and, instead of trying to make them go away, uses them as points of access to meanings present but not overt in the discourse. This technique of reading is derived from the practice of psychoanalysis, and it is in fact indispensable if we are to discover the unconscious motivations of Don Quixote's behavior. What we are looking for is something we can see that betrays the presence of something we can't see, something hidden below the surface of the discourse, or in the terms we have been using, below the level of consciousness. Let's return for a moment to my doubly motivated behavior of always buying Fords. Suppose my Fords begin to break down, causing me expense and aggravation, and yet I refuse to consider buying any other kind of car. At this point there has opened up a gap in my discourse, a discrepancy between what I profess to believe and what is actually happening. My stated motivation no longer explains my behavior. The Fords are clearly not well built and not good value. Continuing to buy them has become self-destructive. Only at this point, when my reasoning contradicts my behavior, can it occur to me or to anyone else that maybe I don't buy the Fords for the reason I think I do. Psychoanalysis has discovered that the slips of the tongue, lapses of memory, inexplicable inconsistencies in reasoning, and so on that we all engage in are the visible indications that something has been repressed, banished from consciousness, or censored out of our discourse. This repressed material or "censored chapter" is precisely what we want to dis-cover, so we are well advised to pay particular attention to the details that don't make sense.

Focusing on these details raises some interesting questions. What does it mean that Don Quixote believes he is in love with Aldonza, when she is so clearly different from other women we have actually seen him fall in love with? And if even thinking about Aldonza causes him so much discomfort that he has to change her into an unapproachable princess named Dulcinea, why does he in I:25 give the secret away to Sancho, allow him to make the connection, and let him describe Aldonza in such an unflattering way without contradicting him? And is it reasonable to fall hopelessly in love with someone you've seen only four times in twelve years, especially if she's as unattractive as Aldonza? These questions at the very least ought to set us to thinking about the relationship between Don Quixote and Aldonza. They suggest that maybe he is not in love with her at all. But solving the riddle of Aldonza only raises another question. If he isn't in love with her, who is he in love with? And by the way, what happened to the question of why he reads so avidly, if it's not to put Aldonza out of his mind?

It has recently been suggested that Don Quixote throws himself into his reading simply because his life is so dull that he has to escape into an imaginary world of sex and violence in order to retain his sanity. This is a plausible hypothesis; we know how deadening his routine is. But we can reasonably suppose that his routine has been the same for years, and the text begins with the narration of his sudden flight into psychosis. Something must have happened to precipitate it. Perhaps the boredom induced by the routine gradually reached a level where it became intolerable. Perhaps, but not necessarily. In any case, we have now seen two quite reasonable hypotheses that reverse the traditionally held relationship between Don Quixote's reading and his madness. He doesn't go crazy because he reads the books; he reads the books in an effort to keep from going crazy. Reading is thus a defense against environmental pressure, a defense that proves inadequate and has to be abandoned. It still remains to determine the exact nature of the environmental pressure.

When Don Quixote sets out on his first sally he addresses Dulcinea *in absentia,* commending himself to her (of course) and also holding her responsible for his departure from home. "O Princess Dulcinea," he begins, "lady of this captive heart, a grievous wrong hast thou done me to drive me forth with scorn, and with inexorable obduracy banish me from the presence of thy beauty" (30). This sentence is a gold mine of unspoken motivation. There is something here that doesn't jibe, another one of those anomalous details that ought to put us on the alert. If Dulcinea is really Aldonza, she couldn't have banished Don Quixote "from the presence of her beauty" because she lives in El Toboso and he lives somewhere else. He wasn't in the presence of her beauty. If Aldonza didn't want him around, or if he didn't want her around, all he would have had to do to avoid her is stay at home. But he does the exact opposite. This contradictory behavior renders the "Aldonza hypothesis" untenable. Don Quixote's flight from home simply can't be a flight from Aldonza, but it is clearly a flight from home. Obviously, something or somebody at home has brought massive, intolerable pressure to bear on Don Quixote, to the point where losing himself in his reading is no longer enough, and he has to get out of there physically, to put real distance between himself and whatever (or whoever) is bothering him.

We come back to the idea that the stultifying routine of Don Quixote's humdrum life has finally driven him mad, but there is another possibility to consider. In light of what we know about men in midlife and their propensity for falling in love with younger women, and considering what we know about Don Quixote's attraction to the innkeeper's daughter (I:16) and to Altisidora (II:44), it might not be unreasonable to think that his niece, who has ripened into a young woman before his eyes over the last couple of years, is somehow responsible for his precipitous departure. There are serious problems with this hypothesis. For one thing, the text hardly mentions the niece, and it doesn't say anywhere that Don Quixote is sexually attracted to her. For another, the very idea that a respectable character in a Classic of World Literature could be motivated by the desire to commit incest (or the even stronger desire to avoid committing incest) seems somehow unworthy, or not nice, or something. In answer to our first objection we can cite the general phenomenon of gaps in the discourse, which we have already examined. And we have seen that this particular text is riddled with gaps and inconsistencies. Don Quixote has seen Aldonza only four times in twelve years, she's ugly and masculine; he is attracted to women who aren't like her; he says she has banished him from her presence, but he wasn't in her presence to start with. These inconsistencies mean that there is literally more here than meets the eye. They mean there is something very important that is not allowed to get into the text precisely because it's unworthy, or not nice, or shameful. These things don't appear in the text for the simple reason that they can't; they are censored out. In response to the business about incest being not nice, we should consider that only those subjects that move us deeply, that bother us, threaten us, engage us (to use Cervantes's word), become the subjects of great literature. And a subject so bothersome that it cannot be talked about openly surely must be important. If that subject is incest, we come back to Aristotle telling us that fictional characters should be "people like ourselves" and then holding up Oedipus as an example. In short, once we notice the inconsistencies in the text and begin to try to explain them, we are driven back to Don Quixote's household and to locate the intolerable environmental stress that has driven him to psychosis precisely there. The only kind of stress powerful enough to call forth a response as drastic as psychosis is something like the threat of incest. The gradual accumulation of boredom, for example, pales beside it.

For me, the only verisimilar explanation for Don Quixote's sudden flight into psychosis is the massive pressure exerted on him by his niece's emergence as a desirable young woman at precisely the worst time in his life, when he is reliving the unresolved psychosexual conflicts of an earlier period. I am led to this conclusion by a particular strategy of reading which I have either adopted or has been forced upon me because of who I am. I begin with the assumption that great characters in literature, the ones worth concerning ourselves about, are "people like ourselves." I further assume this to mean that they have an interior dimension and that their behavior, like ours, is determined simultaneously by conscious and unconscious motivations. The search for unconscious motivations leads me to pay particular attention to the inconsistencies in the logic of the discourse, those gaps that reveal that something has been left out. Combining what I know about real people, in this case men in midlife, with the discovery that there is more here than meets the eye, leads me to formulate the hypothesis I have just presented to explain the etiology of Don Quixote's psychosis. This in turn invites me, maybe even forces me, to read the rest of the text in a certain way, paying particular attention to Don Quixote's relations with women. I read his adventures as the story of how he attempts to dominate his paradoxical combination of terror of women and attraction to them.

I am struck by Don Quixote's empathy with Marcela (I:12–14), who has fled from her home and turned her life into a piece of literature just as he has. Not only does he recognize in her a kind of soul mate, retreating from the pressures of reality into a life-style predetermined by literature, he also seems to find her attractive himself. Why shouldn't he? All the other men desire her, and in addition, she is the same age and in the same kind of family situation as his niece. It is not hard for him to see his niece in her. When he comes forward as her champion and forbids the other men to follow her into the mountains or otherwise interfere with her, he is in effect forbidding himself to do those very things.

We have already seen how Don Quixote is simultaneously attracted to the innkeeper's daughter and terrified by the possibility of actual contact with her in I:16. He is hard at work on an erotic fantasy about her when, so he thinks, she suddenly presents herself at his bedside. (It isn't Don Quixote's fault that she turns out to be Maritornes.) In order to insulate himself from his own desire, he invokes his prior commitment to Dulcinea, but not before regaling himself with the experience of her appearance, her perfume, "and her other charms." The next day he brags to Sancho that he and the lady had spent hours "in amorous colloquies."

People, Real and Fictional

In I:29 Don Quixote makes the acquaintance of the beauteous Dorotea, in the role of Princess Micomicona. She has the same effect on him as the other young women we have already discussed. Their relationship begins with an unsettling embrace. Then Dorotea offers, or pretends to offer, to marry Don Quixote after he kills Pandafilando de la Fosca Vista and restores her kingdom to her. He is at first overjoyed, but almost immediately his fear of intimacy reasserts itself and he begins to back away. He invokes both his loyalty to Dulcinea and his unsuitability for marriage. "You are free to dispose of your person as you like," he tells her, "because as long as I have my memory occupied, my will captivated and my intellect abandoned to that woman . . . I say no more. And it is not possible for me to face the thought of marriage" (I:30). Here the terror of marriage seems stronger than the attachment to Dulcinea, who remains unnamed. It is possible that he doesn't name Dulcinea here because he is thinking of his niece, in which case the impossibility of marriage takes on a new resonance. Sancho finally gets him out of this mess by making an unfavorable comparison between Dorotea and Dulcinea (who for him is Aldonza), whereupon Don Quixote flies into a rage and turns his attention to describing Dulcinea. The crisis has passed.

On the way to Grisóstomo's funeral Don Quixote falls in with a traveler named Vivaldo who realizes he is a madman and asks him a series of leading questions about knight errantry in general. Instead of defining chivalry in terms of armor and battles and searches for the Grail, Don Quixote focuses on the adulterous love affair of Queen Guinevere and Sir Lancelot, which he evokes on several other occasions as well. Similarly, when he is trying to convince the canon from Toledo of the artistic superiority of the romances of chivalry (I:50), he makes up and narrates an episode he considers typical of the genre. We might expect it to be the story of two knights in bloody combat, but instead it is an erotic fantasy about a knight who plunges into a roiling lake. He sinks to the bottom and discovers a crystalline palace there. A "goodly number of damsels" comes trooping out to meet him. They take him inside, where their leader "makes him strip as bare as when his mother bore him." After he is bathed and perfumed, he is dressed and taken to a sumptuous banquet. "And then, when the repast is over, there enters a damsel far more beautiful than any of the others and, seating herself beside him. . . ." Don Quixote's narrative breaks off here, leaving the reader to supply the rest from his own fantasy.

Toward the end of part I Don Quixote hears the story of Eugenio, his friend Anselmo, and Leandra, the woman they both love. She had run away with a soldier who took her money and abandoned her. She has now retreated into a convent. Don Quixote naturally offers to liberate her and, somewhat surprisingly, to turn her over to Eugenio "so that you can use her according to your entire will and pleasure." If we have been attentive to Don Quixote's attitudes toward women throughout the text, this ill-concealed fantasy of sexual domination should not really surprise us.

In part II, as we know, control of the creation of Dulcinea passes from Don Quixote to Sancho. As we also know, Don Quixote gets it back, at least partially, in his dream in the Cave of Montesinos (II:22). In his dream he sees the "enchanted" Dulcinea Sancho had proposed to him back in II:10. This means that Sancho's Dulcinea has percolated down to the preconscious level of Don Quixote's psyche, where dreams are made. She can now stand in for the niece who is still buried at some deeper level. In addition to being enchanted, "Dulcinea" is needy. Her "lady in waiting" asks Don Quixote for a loan of six *reales,* offering a skirt as collateral. He gives her all he has, which is only four *reales.* This is an interesting variation on the basic theme. Here Don Quixote evokes a doubly mediated relationship with Dulcinea (transformed into Sancho's farm girl, who then sends her friend to talk to him), and what assaults him now is a fantasy of impotence. The fear of not having what is required when the moment of truth arrives may be just a manifestation of middle-aged insecurity, but it is also another barrier Don Quixote erects between his desire and the threat of having to act on it. He makes action impossible.

At the duke's palace Don Quixote is offered the opportunity to act out his conflicted sexual desires with a series of real women. The first of these is the duchess herself. When Don Quixote first sees her he practically falls out of his saddle (II:30). When he is ushered into her presence he extends himself in praise of her beauty so much that the duke finally has to remind him that he is pledged to Dulcinea.

The duchess's head *dueña,* Doña Rodríguez, is one of the great minor characters in literature. Because she actually comes to believe in all the deliberate playacting going on around her, and that Don Quixote really is a knight who can restore her daughter's lost honor, she isn't generally studied as one of the women in his life. It is worth considering her in this light, however. She is defined from the start as a middle-aged woman who is very much absorbed in trying to deny her own advancing age and its effect upon her beauty and her sexuality. That is, she presents a kind of feminine counterpart of Don Quixote's masculine midlife crisis. When she enters his room in the middle of the night (II:48), she is coming to ask him to be her daughter's champion, but he believes she is there on behalf of Altisidora. She immediately disabuses him. In fact, she is insulted that he should cast her in the role of go-between, when she thinks she is better suited to be a protagonist. This exchange has the effect of turning their meeting into an erotic encounter. They both begin to fear for their chastity. Don Quixote wraps himself up in the blankets, and Doña Rodríguez approaches his bed with great caution. The scene is played for laughs, but as an episode in Don Quixote's life it borders on tragedy. By virtue of her age and her social class, Doña Rodríguez is the kind of woman Don Quixote should have courted and married when he was younger. His midnight encounter with her is as close as he ever comes to physical intimacy with any woman. If he and Doña Rodríguez could only see each other as people and fall in love, his psychosexual problems would be resolved. The fact that the two of them do not become intimate is a poignant reminder of how far Don Quixote's problems really are from being resolved.

The object of our hero's affections while he is the duke's guest is of course not the fiftyish Doña Rodríguez but the young and beautiful Altisidora. She pretends to be in love with him, and he throws himself into reciprocating, only his feelings are genuine. Altisidora in part II is like the innkeeper's daughter in part I, a young woman in whom he sees the image of his niece, and with whom he falls hopelessly in love because he is already in love with the niece. He immediately invokes his prior commitment to Dulcinea as a barrier between his desire and his terror of it. What is unique to his experience with Altisidora is that she is drawn into his feelings, and the relationship evolves. That is, she seems to be not entirely playacting when she pretends to love him. When he summons up all his strength and attempts to deflect her advances, he becomes more attractive to her. Altisidora is a typical character in part II, in the sense that she begins something as a game and before long she is vitally involved in it. All this comes out in II:70 when Don Quixote and Sancho pass through the duke's domains a second time, on their way back to La Mancha after the disastrous events in Barcelona. Altisidora declares herself to him once again, and he finds himself able to reject her without an inner struggle. Somehow, perhaps because of his recent defeat in battle, perhaps just through the passage of time, he has been cured of his infatuation. His rejection of her is serene and final, and it provokes a violent response from her. In fact, the particular vehemence of her verbal attack on him is one of those inconsistencies that signals the presence of something hidden below the level of the discourse. That something is Altisidora's true feelings for Don Quixote. The duke, of all people, sees through her rhetorical overkill. "That reminds me," he says after she unleashes a barrage of insults, "of the common saying, that 'the lover who says hurtful things is ready to forgive' " (813). Altisidora's story might begin here as Don Quixote rides out of her life forever, but the book is about him. From his point of view, his experience with Altisidora has allowed him to work through and overcome his feelings toward his niece. When he is cured of Altisidora he is also cured of that other woman Altisidora represents. He can go home now and face his niece in a different way.

My Don Quixote is a sexual being, whose identity, whose story, and whose interest for me as a reader ultimately depend on his sexuality. My Don Quixote is propelled backward into life by his flight from an unbearable environmental pressure personified in his niece and the threat of incest. It is because of this that he first throws himself into the reading of romances of chivalry. When this first line of defense proves inadequate, the only mental space left to retreat into is madness. Similarly, the physical space of his house has become so erotically charged as to be uninhabitable. He absents himself mentally by losing touch with reality, and he has to get out physically as well. In order to do this he conceives the project of reviving knight-errantry, teams up with Sancho and enters into the most moving and humanly valuable relationship that either man ever engages in. His existence as mad Don Quixote is clearly more interesting and valuable than his prequixotic state as an anonymous rural hidalgo. This existence comes to an end, as I read the book, when he has finally resolved his unacceptable attraction toward his niece in the course of his second sojourn at the duke and duchess's. In his infatuation with Altisidora he acts out his desire for his niece, and when he is cured of Altisidora, he can go home and face the niece, no longer the object of forbidden desire. Freed from his desire, he no longer feels the need to be Don Quixote. Furthermore, the life he comes home to is the drab routine of a country hidalgo, and when his housekeeper counsels him to be like Don Diego de Miranda, he just can't take any more. He retreats once more, into the only space remaining for him, a transitory new identity and death.

Many readers find it impossible to accompany me in this reading. Lots of them are offended by the idea that a harmless old crazy like Don Quixote could harbor sexual desire for any woman, let alone his own niece. Many people are offended by the thought of incest, period. Some readers do not consider Don Quixote to be a complex, verisimilar character at all, but a puppet manipulated by a satirist, to engage in social criticism, or to tell us how not to read. Many other readers simply prefer to look at other themes. They keep the social history of Cervantes's Spain, or chivalry, or Don Quixote's relation to the knights of yore, or the book's relation to other books, in the foreground of their attention. Many others lose themselves in the fascinating questions of contemporary critical theory that Cervantes seems to have anticipated. Perhaps they do this because they are too troubled by their own sexuality to consider Don Quixote as a sexual being. Perhaps not. The preferred themes are perfectly legitimate and very interesting, after all.

Maybe I'm the oddball here. It has been demonstrated, and I have no choice but to agree, that the etiology of Don Quixote's madness is narrated in perfect accord with the most advanced sixteenth-century theories of personality and character disorders, in particular the *Examen de ingenios* (Examination of men's wits, 1575) of Dr. Juan Huarte de San Juan. Huarte offers a physiological explanation based on the ancient belief in the imbalance among the four bodily fluids, or humors, as the determinant of personality. Nowhere does he consider the threat of incest or any other environmental pressure. Maybe I read as I do because I have sex on the brain. That's perfectly possible too. Cervantes tells us over and over in a hundred ways that when we read, we read ourselves. As Sansón Carrasco puts it, "opinions differ because people's tastes are not the same."

Notes

1. James Iffland, "On the Social Destiny of *Don Quixote:* Literature and Ideological Interpellation," *Journal of the Midwest Modern Language Association* 20.1 (1987): 17–36, 20.2 (1987): 9–27.

2. Marthe Robert, *The Old and the New* (Berkeley and Los Angeles: University of California Press, 1977), 5–6.

3. This citation and the other quotations in this paragraph are from Peter E. Russell, "*Don Quixote* as a Funny Book," *Modern Language Review* 64 (1969): 312–26.

4. See also Anthony J. Close, *The Romantic Approach to "Don Quixote"* (Cambridge: Cambridge University Press, 1977), and Daniel Eisenberg, *A Study of "Don Quixote" in which Cervantes' Goals in "Don Quixote" are Examined. With Index and Copious Notes* (Newark, Del.: Juan de la Cuesta, 1987). John G. Weiger concludes that the book's initial reception as a work of humor is "an undisputed fact" in *The Substance of Cervantes* (Cambridge: Cambridge University Press, 1985), 26.

5. Quoted by Américo Castro in "An Introduction to the *Quijote*," in Stephen Gilman and Edmund King, *An Idea of History: Selected Essays of Ameérico Castro* (Columbus: Ohio State University Press, 1977), 77–139.

6. Friedrich Wilhelm von Schelling, *Philosophie der Kunst* (Philosophy of art) (1802). Cited in Castro, "An Introduction," 82, and Close, *Romantic Approach*, 33.

7. Iffland, "Social Destiny," part 2, p. 12

8. Arthur Efron, *Don Quixote and the Dulcineated World* (Austin: University of Texas Press, 1971), 4.

9. Alban Forcione, *Cervantes, Aristotle and the Persiles* (Princeton: Princeton University Press, 1970), *Cervantes' Christian Romance: A Study of "Persiles y Sigismunda"* (Princeton: Princeton University Press, 1972), *Cervantes and the Humanist Vision: A Study of Four Exemplary Novels* (Princeton: Princeton University Press, 1982), and *Cervantes and the Mystery of Lawless-*

ness: A Study of "El casamiento engañoso y El coloquio de los perros" (Princeton: Princeton University Press, 1984).

10. Joaquín Casalduero, *Sentido y forma del Quijote 1605–1615* (Madrid: Ediciones Insula, 1949).

11. John G. Weiger, *The Individuated Self: Cervantes and the Emergence of the Individual* (Athens, Ohio: Ohio University Press, 1979).

12. C. B. Johnson, *Madness and Lust: A Psychoanalytical Approach to Don Quixote* (Berkeley and Los Angeles: University of California Press, 1983).

13. Ruth El Saffar, *Beyond Fiction: The Recovery of the Feminine in the Novels of Cervantes* (Berkeley and Los Angeles: University of California Press, 1984).

14. Louis Combet, *Cervantès ou les incertitudes du désir* (Lyon: Presses Universitaires de Lyon, 1980).

15. Américo Castro, *España en su historia: cristianos, moros y judíos* (Buenos Aires: Losada, 1948); revised edition translated as *The Structure of Spanish History* (Princeton: Princeton University Press, 1954).

16. Francisco Márquez Villanueva, *Fuentes literarias cervantinas* (Madrid: Gredos, 1973); *Personajes y temas del Quijote* (Madrid: Taurus, 1975). Joseph Silverman, "Sancho Panza y su secretario," *Tribuna Israelita* (Mexico) 31, no. 319 (1975): 38–42; and "Saber vidas ajenas: un tema de vida y literatura y sus variantes cervantinas," *Papeles de Son Armadans* 167 (1973): 197–212.

17. Efron, *Don Quixote*, 5.

18. Ibid., 4–5.

19. Daniel Eisenberg, *Castilian Romances of Chivalry in the Sixteenth Century: A Bibliography* (London: Grant and Cutler, 1979), *Romances of Chivalry in the Spanish Golden Age* (Newark, Del.: Juan de la Cuesta, 1982), and *A Study*. Edwin Williamson, *The Halfway House of Fiction: Don Quixote and Arthurian Romance* (Oxford: Clarendon Press, 1984).

20. Ruth El Saffar, *Distance and Control in "Don Quixote": A Study in Narrative Technique* (Chapel Hill: University of North Carolina Press, 1975), and *Beyond Fiction* (1985).

21. Norman Holland, "Unity Identity Text Self," in *Reader-Response Criticism from Formalism to Post-Structuralism,* ed. Jane P. Tompkins (Baltimore: Johns Hopkins University Press, 1980), 118–33.

22. Louis Althusser, "Ideology and Ideological State Apparatuses (Notes toward an Investigation)," in *"Lenin and Philosophy" and Other Essays* (New York: Monthly Review Press, 1971). Quoted in Iffland, "Social Destiny," part 1, p. 22.

Bibliography

Primary Works

Two readily accessible editions of the Spanish text, with informative introductions and helpful notes in Spanish:

Don Quijote. 2 vols. Edited by John Jay Allen. Madrid: Cátedra, 1976.

Don Quijote. 3 vols. Edited by Luis Andrés Murillo. Madrid: Castalia, 1978. Volume 3 is *Bibliografía fundamental*.

The most useful English translation:

Don Quixote. The Ormsby translation, revised. Edited by Joseph R. Jones and Kenneth Douglas. New York: W.W. Norton, 1981. In addition to an accurate and readable translation, this edition contains excerpts from important literary texts (*Amadís de Gaula*, *Orlando furioso*, etc.) and ten particularly relevant critical essays.

Other usable versions:

Don Quixote. Translated by Samuel Putnam. New York: The Viking Press, 1949. This is also the "Modern Library" version.

The Adventures of Don Quixote. Translated by J. M. Cohen. Baltimore: Penguin, 1963.

Secondary Works

Biographies

Astrana Marín, Luis. *Vida heroica y ejemplar de Miguel de Cervantes Saavedra*. 7 vols. Madrid: Instituto Editorial Reus, 1948–1958. The most scholarly; based entirely on documents, which are reproduced. In Spanish.

Canavaggio, Jean. *Cervantès*. Paris: Mazarine, 1986. In French. Spanish translation, Madrid: Espasa-Calpe, 1987. The most up-to-date; winner of an important prize in France.

Predmore, Richard L. *Cervantes*. New York: Dodd, Mead and Co., 1973. Very readable. Interesting illustrations.

Anthologies of Criticism

Avalle-Arce, Juan Bautista, and E. C. Riley, eds. *Suma cervantina*. London: Támesis Books, 1973. Essays by Asensio, Bataillon, Moreno Báez, Riquer, Wardropper, and others, as well as the editors. A generally conservative vision. In Spanish.

Bjornson, Richard, ed. *Approaches to Teaching Cervantes' "Don Quixote."* New York: The Modern Language Association, 1984. A stimulating variety of current American approaches.

El Saffar, Ruth, ed. *Critical Essays on Cervantes*. Boston: G.K. Hall, 1986. Classic studies, including pertinent excerpts from books by Michel Foucault and Marthe Robert.

Flores, Angel, and M. J. Benardete, eds. *Cervantes Across the Centuries*. New York: Dryden Press, 1947; rpt. New York: Gordian Press, 1969. Fundamental essays by Casalduero, Castro, Spitzer, and others.

Haley, George, ed. *El Quijote de Cervantes*. Madrid: Taurus, 1980. Essays by European and American hispanists, organized by literary problem, e.g. intertextuality. In Spanish.

McGaha, Michael D., ed. *Cervantes and the Renaissance*. Easton, Pa.: Juan de la Cuesta, 1980. Papers from a 1978 symposium by Allen, Avalle-Arce, Durán, El Saffar, Murillo, Rivers, and others.

Nelson, Lowry, Jr., ed. *Cervantes, a Collection of Critical Essays*. Englewood Cliffs, N.J.: Prentice-Hall, 1969. Essays by international critics and writers, including Harry Levin and Thomas Mann.

Classic and Recent *Quixote* Studies

Allen, John J. *Don Quixote, Hero or Fool? A Study in Narrative Technique*. 2 vols. Gainesville: University of Florida Press, 1969, 1979. Studies the pattern of Don Quixote's successes and failures. Very useful discussion of narrative voice and textual rhetoric.

Avalle-Arce, Juan Bautista. *Deslindes cervantinos*. Madrid; Edhigar, 1961. Intelligent essays on various aspects of Cervantes and his works. In Spanish.

Bibliography

———. *Don Quijote como forma de vida*. Madrid: Fundación Juan March/ Editorial Castalia, 1976. Vigorous "existential" reading. In Spanish.

Casalduero, Joaquín. *Sentido y forma del Quijote*. Madrid: Ediciones Insula, 1949, rpt. 1966, 1970. Structural analysis in terms of the categories of art history. In Spanish.

Castro, Américo. *El pensamiento de Cervantes* (1925). Nueva edición ampliada y con notas del autor y de Julio Rodríguez Puértolas. Barcelona, Madrid: Editorial Noguer, 1972. Situates Cervantes in Renaissance intellectual history and, in the revised edition, in Spanish social history as well. In Spanish.

———. *Cervantes y los casticismos españoles*. Madrid: Alfaguara, 1966. Strongest argument in favor of Cervantes's *converso* background and social marginality. In Spanish.

———. *Hacia Cervantes*. 3d ed. Madrid: Taurus, 1967. Essays on Cervantes and his social and intellectual milieu. In Spanish.

———. "An Introduction to the *Quijote*," in *An Idea of History: Selected Essays of Américo Castro*, edited by Stephen Gilman and Edmund L. King, 77–144. Columbus: Ohio State University Press, 1977. Concise statement of Castro's views on Spanish social history and the themes of the *Quixote*. Awkward translation.

Close, Anthony J. *The Romantic Approach to "Don Quixote": A Critical History of the Romantic Tradition in "Quixote" Criticism*. Cambridge: Cambridge University Press, 1977. Debunks "symbolistic" readings. Excellent history of critical reception since the eighteenth century.

Combet, Louis. *Cervantès ou les incertitudes du désir*. Lyon: Presses Universitaires de Lyon, 1980. A "psycho-structural" approach, with special emphasis on sadomasochism and sexual ambiguity. In French.

Durán, Manuel. *La ambigüedad en el Quijote*. Xalapa: Universidad Veracruzana, 1960. Probably the most cogent "perspectivist" reading. In Spanish.

Efron, Arthur. *Don Quixote and the Dulcineated World*. Austin: University of Texas Press, 1971. Cervantes as unwitting spokesman for the forces of reaction. Good discussion of critical approaches.

Eisenberg, Daniel. *A Study of "Don Quixote," in Which Cervantes' Goals in Don Quixote are Examined. With Index and Copious Notes*. Newark, Del.: Juan de la Cuesta, 1987. A "hard-line" reading that turns "soft" at the end. Massive documentation on chivalric romance in Spain.

El Saffar, Ruth. *Distance and Control in "Don Quixote": A Study in Narrative Technique*. Chapel Hill: University of North Carolina Press, 1975. Perceptive discussion of narrative poetics. Ahead of its time in Hispanic studies.

————. *Beyond Fiction: The Recovery of the Feminine in the Novels of Cervantes*. Berkeley and Los Angeles: University of California Press, 1984. Stimulating discussion of Cervantes's presentation of women from a Jungian perspective.

Johnson, Carroll B. *Madness and Lust: A Psychoanalytical Approach to "Don Quixote."* Berkeley and Los Angeles: University of California Press, 1983. Don Quixote and midlife crisis.

Madariaga, Salvador de. *"Don Quixote": An Introductory Essay in Psychology*. Oxford: Clarendon Press, 1935. Revised ed. 1961. Perceptive character analyses.

Mancing, Howard. *The Chivalric World of "Don Quixote": Style, Structure, and Narrative Technique*. Columbia, Mo.: University of Missouri Press, 1982. The institution of chivalry and its relation to Don Quixote's self-concept.

Márquez Villanueva, Francisco. *Personajes y temas del Quijote*. Madrid: Taurus, 1975. Extraordinarily erudite and sensitive essays on several much-discussed episodes. In Spanish.

Murillo, Luis A. *A Critical Introduction to "Don Quixote."* New York: Peter Lang, 1988. Chapter-by-chapter analysis of relation of Don Quixote to exemplarity, to fiction, to myth. Good discussion of chivalry.

Ortega y Gasset, José. *Meditations on Quixote*. Introduction and notes by Julián Marías. New York: W.W. Norton, 1961. The notion of "perspective."

Parr, James A. *"Don Quixote": An Anatomy of Subversive Discourse*. Newark, Del.: Juan de la Cuesta, 1988. Up-to-date discussion of authorial voices and presences.

Predmore, Richard L. *The World of Don Quixote*. Cambridge: Harvard University Press, 1967. Excellent analysis of the functions of literature. Rewarding.

Reed, Walter L. *An Exemplary History of the Novel: The Quixotic versus the Picaresque*. Chicago: University of Chicago Press, 1981. Excellent discussion of the centrality of *Don Quixote*.

Riley, Edward C. *Cervantes's Theory of the Novel*. Oxford: Clarendon Press, 1964. Cervantes and Aristotelian poetics. Informative.

————. *Don Quixote*. London: Allen and Unwin, 1986. An introduction similar to the present book, but written for the British reader and more concerned with questions of literary genre.

Spitzer, Leo. "Linguistic Perspectivism in *Don Quixote*," in *Linguistics and Literary History*, 41–85. Princeton: Princeton University Press, 1967. Anticipates Michel Foucault's analysis of the new relation between word and thing in the *Quixote*.

Bibliography

Weiger, John G. *The Individuated Self: Cervantes and the Emergence of the Individual.* Athens, Ohio: Ohio University Press, 1979. A Jungian-existentialist analysis.

————. *The Substance of Cervantes.* Cambridge: Cambridge University Press, 1985. Excellent exposition of Cervantes's self-awareness. Cervantes has always managed to be ahead of his readers.

Williamson, Edwin. *The Halfway House of Fiction: "Don Quixote" and Arthurian Romance.* Oxford: Clarendon Press, 1984. One of the more sophisticated discussions of chivalric romance.

Willis, Raymond S., Jr. *The Phantom Chapters of the Quijote.* New York: The Hispanic Institute of America, 1953. Perceptive analysis of the relation of action to formal structure.

Index

Index

Index

About the Author

A native of Los Angeles, Carroll B. Johnson was educated at UCLA and Harvard (Ph.D., 1966). Since 1964 he has been a member of the Department of Spanish and Portuguese at UCLA. He was for six years its chairman, "where he learned to have patience in adversity." Professor Johnson is the author of three books on narrative fiction, including *Madness and Lust: A Psychoanalytical Approach to "Don Quixote"* (1983), and of articles and reviews in several scholarly journals.